enough!

★ Audio Recording ★

The meditations in this book are designed to develop familiarity
with states of mind that can release us from addictive patterns.
These meditations have been recorded by Chönyi Taylor
as a supplement to *Enough!* Please check the Snow Lion
Publications website for availability: www.snowlionpub.com

enough!

A Buddhist Approach to Finding Release
from Addictive Patterns

Chönyi Taylor

SNOW LION PUBLICATIONS
ITHACA, NEW YORK

Snow Lion Publications
P. O. Box 6483
Ithaca, NY 14851 USA
(607) 273-8519
www.snowlionpub.com

Printed in USA on acid-free recycled paper.

ISBN-10: 1-55939-344-0
ISBN-13: 978-1-55939-344-7

Library of Congress Cataloging-in-Publication Data

Taylor, Chönyi, 1942–
  Enough! : a Buddhist approach to finding release from
addictive patterns / Chönyi Taylor.
    p. cm.
  Includes bibliographical references and index.
  ISBN-13: 978-1-55939-344-7 (alk. paper)
  ISBN-10: 1-55939-344-0 (alk. paper)
  1. Twelve-step programs—Religious aspects—Buddhism.
  2. Compulsive behavior—Religious aspects—Buddhism.
  3. Habit breaking—Religious aspects—Buddhism.
  4. Spiritual life—Buddhism. 5. Self-help techniques.
  I. Title. II. Title: Buddhist approach to finding release from
addictive patterns. BQ4570.T85T39 2010
    294.3'4442—dc22   2009053963

Designed and typeset by Gopa & Ted2, Inc.

contents

Appendices

list of meditations

acknowledgments

THERE ARE countless people who have directly or indirectly helped me put this book together. It began as a request from people who felt they benefited from my workshops on addiction. My gratitude to those people, and to Michael Davies, who pushed me into doing the workshops in the first place.

My gratitude, also, to those people who helped and encouraged me through the various obstacles one meets in writing a book. On the professional side, Eng Kong Tan, Bruno Cayoun, Brian Gutkin, Maris Depers, and Antonio Tejero Pociello assured me that my work would be helpful to their clients. Margot-Deepa Slater gave invaluable feedback from the point of view of a recovered addict. Nancy Patton has unfailingly mothered me through my various crises and self-doubts as well as giving me editorial assistance. To Sue Ford (1943-2009), friend extraordinaire and constant supporter, may you receive in your next life what you had given in this one.

My editors at Snow Lion have been unfailingly kind and helpful. Special thanks to Susan Kyser for her wise advice.

Then there are my friends and family, Buddhist and non-Buddhist, who have always been on hand during glumness or glee. My children, Susan, Liz, and James, keep my feet on the ground and my grandchildren even more so.

My Buddhist background has developed principally under the kindness and guidance of Lama Zopa Rinpoche, Geshe Doga, Geshe Tashi Tsering, and Geshe Samten. Any mistakes are due to my own limitations and not due to the quality and depth of their teachings.

We are all addicted, to a greater or lesser degree, to something.

The most insidious addiction is not drug related, but our addiction to our own self-pity and small mindedness. If this book helps anyone, even a little, then I have achieved my aim.

Chönyi Taylor
Sandy Point, Australia
July 2009

introduction

*Do not expect material objects to satisfy you or to make your life perfect;
it's impossible. How can you be satisfied with even vast amounts of
material objects? How will sleeping with hundreds of people satisfy you?
It will never happen. Satisfaction comes from the mind.*
—LAMA YESHE[1]

THIS IS a book for people who have had enough: people who
want to change those addictive patterns and thoughts which
range from being mildly annoying to threatening our physical and
mental health and even our lives. It is a book for people who are
willing to take responsibility and make some effort to change. It is a
book for people who would like to have self-confidence, hope, and
courage instead of the damaging effects of addiction. This is a book
for strengthening the power of our own minds as the key tool for
changing addictive patterns. This is a book based on Buddhist teachings, but the ideas are relevant to anyone, regardless of their religion, who wishes to reclaim their humanity and spiritual awareness.

If we wish to escape addiction and avoid relapse, the most important factor is not what we are addicted to, but the state of our minds.
We all have addictions, big or little. Many of these little addictions
are more insidious than drug and alcohol addictions. We might, for
example, be addicted to our own point of view, causing unnecessary harm through bigotry or hypocrisy. We might be addicted to
feeling useless. We might be addicted to coming in first, or never
trying because it is all too hard. We might be addicted to getting
people to say nice things about us, or making them angry with us
so we can blame them for our misery. These inner addictions are

much harder to identify and change than the outer addictions, but they are more important. In the end, we are addicted to our own self-pity. That is why we boost our ego with bravado or crumple under the pressure of feeling bad, which in turn is why we hang on to small mindedness and blaming others. Then we find ourselves alone, with little to love and few people who love us. We are deeply and painfully unhappy at that stage. In the end, that is why we try to find happiness through something which stops us thinking about such things and leaves us, for the moment, feeling okay.

If we want to be free of our addictions, big or little, we have no choice but to work with our own minds. This is not as impossible as it seems. One of the main points about Buddhist teaching is that we can change our minds for the better. What does "better" mean? It simply means being in balance, not being thrown around by the rising and falling of events and experiences. It means we accept the world for what it is and ourselves for what we are without being upset. It means we give up the blame game in favor of checking out why we are unhappy. It means accepting the things we cannot change and doing something about the things we can change, whether these things are inside our heads or outside in our homes and our environment. If we could be "better" in that way, then we would be at peace with ourselves, and that means we would be at peace with the people around us.

All this is nice in theory, but not so easy in the real world. We need some wisdom to know what we can do immediately and tools to train our mind away from the habits behind our addictions. The wisdom side has two aspects. The first is about finding effective tools for change and the second is about knowing what really makes us happy—whether our beliefs about life really do help us to be happy. Happiness is so often related to whether we feel a loving sense of connection with other people and our environment. If we can find ways to develop this profound quality, then we become reconnected with our ability to love and find that we are loved in return. As we search for a lasting happiness, we discover a wisdom that is compassionate and a compassion that is wise.

If we want to make an effort to change, we need to be motivated.

At first the motivation to escape the addiction comes when our fear of the consequences is greater than our fear of being without our addiction. This is when we first say, "Enough!" If we know that change is possible we find the energy to make those changes and actually put the ideas into practice. We do that by understanding that it is possible to change, by understanding what direction that change could take. That direction will follow the values we have chosen for our lives. It makes sense to choose values that are helpful. When we also hear about or meet people who have succeeded where we have not, then we are inspired to follow their path. This inspiration also strengthens our motivation.

When we are in the trap of an addiction, we feel as if choice has been taken away. However, we can reclaim our ability to make choices. Knowing this also helps us to be motivated. As we do so, we reclaim responsibility for our ideas and motivations and actions. We begin to realize that instead of creating suffering for ourselves and other people, we can create kindness and patience. Again we need the two great qualities of wisdom and compassion. At first we find and hold little wisdoms, little nuggets of insights into ourselves and into life. Then we take hold of these nuggets and polish them. We make that wisdom our own.

Why Bother?

Addictive patterns are harmful, not only to us, but often to other people as well. The more we are held in the grip of an addiction, the more we forget about other people. Our lives become increasingly focused around the addiction. We become more and more self-centered, more and more isolated from the world, less and less caring about the effects we are having on everyone. We may become angry with the people who are trying to help us and angry with the world in general. We may become angry with ourselves for not having the strength to break the addiction. These are not happy states of mind.

Addictions are a desperate way of seeking happiness. They take us away from the uncomfortable or miserable or acutely painful reality of our lives. They provide a temporary relief. But like a fly trying to struggle out of a spider's web, each time we seek that relief, instead of finding a way out of our dissatisfactions, we are caught more tightly. There must be a better way to find happiness.

I've Tried Before, but I Fall Back

Whether we agree or disagree with the idea that addiction is an illness, the reasons people relapse after treatment for drug addiction are mostly psychological. These include being unable to cope with emotions like anger, fear, and depression; peer pressure and other social pressures; and conflicts with other people such as parents or partners.[2] If those are the reasons for relapsing, then they are likely to be the reasons for getting addicted in the first place.

For some people the "feeling good" aspect of addiction may be so strong that it is hard to resist. It is also hard for a diabetic to resist sugary foods. The diabetic and the addict both need to be determined to improve things, and that determination comes from the mind, from the way we think, not from the body. If we accept responsibility for the results of our choices, that in itself will strengthen our determination. If we also know that we can overcome the addiction, then we are inspired to change.

What Is Addiction?
Addiction Is Primarily a State of Mind

What happened when we first went shopping or gambling, or took our first drink or cigarette? *We made a decision.* At that time, we did not intend to get addicted to anything. We didn't think that this action would become a compulsion and take over our lives. We liked the feeling of what we did and then wanted more and more. The more often we do something, the more likely it is that it will become a habit. Whatever the pressures on us at that time, we cannot avoid the fact that we made an initial decision, and then lots of additional decisions. So addiction begins with the mind.

The cause of our addiction is not primarily in the substance.

Take the relatively harmless addiction to chocolate. Chocolate sitting on the supermarket shelves does not ask to be taken and eaten. Our actions become a problem after we slip into compulsively buying, unwrapping, and eating the chocolate. The same is also true for alcohol, tobacco, and hard drugs. After some time, the act of buying and consuming the substance becomes a habit. Habits are states of mind and can be changed.

Some of us are addicted to smoking. When did we light our first cigarette and why? To be with the in-group? To lose weight? To calm down? It worked and so we took another cigarette. And another. Not only have we gotten into the group, or lost weight, or calmed down, but we have also altered our body chemistry so that we need more nicotine. The physical changes brought on by smoking or addictions to hard drugs certainly make the addiction harder to overcome, but the fact remains that the addiction is rooted in a state of mind.

Fundamentally the problem is a mental problem. While it is true that external circumstances may make it easier or harder to gratify the addiction of our choice, we cannot avoid the conclusion that the originating cause of our addiction is in our mind. It is also true that if we do not accept responsibility for our addiction, and if we do not see a need to change, then nothing outside will help. The best cure for addiction is also within our own minds.

Addiction Involves Compulsion: It Is a Habit

When we constantly repeat something, it becomes a habit, something done without thinking. We lose the ability to choose because we have forgotten by this stage why we started the habit. We feel we are compelled to act. This feeling of compulsion may be so strong that we do not even know that we are caught in the addiction. We find ourselves already smoking the cigarette, already eating the chocolate, already buying the clothes, already finishing the bottle of whisky, already placing the bet, already high. It seems as though the addiction is out there. It seems to be the fault of the thing that is tempting us. We might even blame our own mind but say, "It's not really me." But we cannot avoid the fact that we are the ones who started this addictive pattern in the first place. It is the habit which has become an addiction that gives the illusion that the addiction is not in our minds but out there somewhere.

Habits in themselves can be quite useful. Once we have developed a habit, then our conscious mind does not need to bother with details. When we get up in the morning we mostly function by habit. We have our routine. We shower, brush our teeth, shave or put on make-up, all without thinking much about it. We get into the car or onto the bus without thinking. A habit enables us to do repetitive things and leaves our minds free for more interesting things. The more deeply ingrained the habit, the less conscious control we seem to have. Overriding a habit is not easy, but it is not impossible.

There Seems to Be No Conscious Control

When we do not have conscious control, then it seems as if the habit has taken over our mind. A good example of this is when we start driving along a familiar route, but this time with a different destination. When we were supposed to take a different turnoff we were lost in our thoughts. Oh, no! We are still on the familiar route. The habit has taken over. What has really happened is that we allowed the habit to function because it has been so useful for most of that route. If we had kept our mind on the task, to get to the unfamiliar place, then we would have overridden the habit. This shows that we can override a habit *if* we keep our mind on the task.

Sometimes, it is difficult to override the habit due to this seeming lack of conscious control. I think of the times when I have driven an automatic car. My car is manual. When I drive an automatic car, my foot looks for the clutch, even when I tell myself not to. I feel uncomfortable and awkward. But if I drive the automatic car for several days and then get back into my manual, the opposite happens. I forget to use the clutch.

Phobias are habits that have taken over in this way. If I have a fear of spiders, then that fear is triggered whenever I see a spider, or even when I think I see a spider. The habit has become so strong that I am caught up in the reaction even before I know for certain whether the shape I can see is really a spider or just a clump of black thread. A strong addiction is like a phobia. When such things as fear or stress or anger demand to be relieved by the addictive substance or behavior, this demand is so strong that we find we are caught in our addictive behavior before we are even aware of the severe discomfort that triggered it.

Obsessive behaviors are also deeply ingrained habits. People caught in an obsession know that what they are doing is not helpful, but they feel they can't make themselves stop. Obsessions, phobias, and habits can all be changed if we have some good methods and choose to put them into practice. We can regain control again through watching our minds and learning to accept our irrational fears. This means understanding and practicing equanimity and mindfulness.

The Immediate Effect of the Addiction Is Pleasant

Even if I just think about chocolate, I experience the special, sweet pleasure of it melting in my mouth. Every time I eat some chocolate I experience that same pleasure. I have discovered something that feels good however bad I might be feeling or however awful my life might be. Drug and alcohol addiction, addictions to food, shopping, sex, gambling, and so on all have short-term pleasures. We forget that we even had problems. The mindlessness of addiction means that we no longer feel any pain. If that pleasurable process is very strong, then the addiction can become very powerful. We all want to feel good. We all want to be happy. For that moment we do feel good, we do feel happy.

Even if you have a habit of hurting yourself in some way, such as nail biting, or pulling out hair, that pain takes over from some other pain. That is a very short-term pleasure, like scratching an itch, which comes through relief of a deeper pain, such as being abused or feeling a failure. The mental addiction to feeling bad is similar. If we focus on how bad we are, then we can forget about other difficulties. We do not have to do anything about them because we are so bad anyway. We give ourselves relief from a deeper pain.

We can undermine the idea that short-term pleasure really gives us what we want by thinking about what makes us happy in the long term. This is part of what it means to develop wisdom.

The Long-Term Effect of the Addiction Is Harmful to Us

Whatever the addiction, in the end it causes a lot of harm to us. This is very clear with alcohol, tobacco, and hard drug addictions. Addictions can be a direct cause of serious illness. Withdrawal can bring serious physical symptoms. Harm comes from other addictions as well. The gambler or the shopaholic has to get money. Too much chocolate means too much weight. Addictive weight loss can lead to organ failure. When we fully realize how damaging our addiction has been, then we want to say, "Enough!" We become stronger in our intention to change. If a habit is not harmful, then there is no reason to change it.

The Addiction Is Harmful to Others

When we are addicted, what we want for ourselves takes priority, and the real needs of others are ignored or trivialized. People who have had to steal or to lie or to hurt someone in order to indulge in their addiction know in their hearts that this is destroying the people they love as well as destroying their own good names and good hearts. This is the source of the shame that usually goes with addiction. The more intensely we feel compelled to indulge in our addictive patterns, the worse this destructive behavior becomes. With any addiction there is the temporary reward that comes about with the addiction itself. We momentarily feel better. The more we feel better, the more we want the pleasurable effects of our addiction. In fact, for the moment, we feel so much better that we do not have to think about other consequences. We become more and more self-centered and self-pitying. We begin to forget that other people have needs too. Whatever our addiction, its impact on the people we love can be devastating. The guilt and shame we feel can be so overwhelming that it can send us back to the addiction. Reconnecting with people who care for us and being mindful of their needs can bring joy and happiness back into our lives.

The Definition

The definition of addiction which is used in this book summarizes the points we have just looked at: Addiction is a mental habit in which there appears to be no conscious control, which gives short-term pleasure and long-term harm, and in which our own needs override the needs of others.

Am I Sick?

Maybe yes and maybe no. Alcoholics Anonymous[3] says that alcoholism is an illness. Not everyone agrees. Not all addictions happen because there is something wrong with our bodies. Medicine helps to rebalance the body, but if the mind is still dissatisfied, then we are likely to head straight back into an addiction.

So What Can We Do?

Unhooking ourselves from our addictive behavior is a slow process. This is partly because changing habits from negative ones to positive ones is slow, but also because it takes time to examine our minds sufficiently to get to the more and more subtle causes of our addictions. This book has been designed to start with the obvious aspects of our addictive patterns and then proceed to more subtle levels.

The first step, of course, is that we need to recognize we have a problem. Without that step, we have no interest in making any changes, so the book assumes that each of us has already decided we want to change.

Next, we become aware of what our mind is doing instead of looking for ways to run away from it. We become mindful instead of mindless. We start to check out the events leading up to our indulging ourselves and our ego—the triggers that set us into the addictive pattern. As we become more aware and mindful, we can start to see that triggers are found at deeper and deeper levels of our mind. We begin to develop an understanding of the causes and effects that apply to those addictions that sit in the recesses of our mind.

If we want to be free from addictions, then we also need to break the tightness of our self-centeredness. Unfortunately selfishness makes the addiction worse. Any time we feel bad, selfishness says thing like, "You have a right to be happy and this addiction will make you happy" or "I can't cope. I need a break because it is all too much for me." If we are to break that cycle, then we need to understand how faulty these justifications can be. It is the self-centered mind that catastrophizes and dramatizes the disasters that will happen if we do not have access to our addiction. Exposing these exaggerations is essential.

We also need to know how and why the habit started in the first place. For example, if I want to stop my shopping sprees, I can cut up my credit cards. That is a start. But if I want to stop the urge to go shopping in the first place, then I need to know why I feel compelled. Then maybe I can find better ways of curbing my shopping habit. Information is power. If I can understand how and why my addictive patterns arose in the first place, then there is the possibility that I can do something to change those patterns. Knowing we can change even the deepest habits gives us hope. Hope gives us energy. This give us the opportunity to create new patterns, new habits.

What else can we do? We will get into more detail as we proceed through the book. Meanwhile there is one more tool which is most important in releasing ourselves from addictive patterns—equanimity

Why Equanimity?

Equanimity is a quality we can develop which helps us to deal with everyday stresses and to stay with and investigate parts of our lives which may be quite painful. Equanimity is an aspect of the mind that notices what happens to us without getting into dramatics. It does not exaggerate events in our lives. It does not get wildly excited at each small change for the better, but notices the change and is happy about it. Equanimity does not get consumed by anger when we do not succeed. It defuses the over-the-top emotions that boil up when we do not get our own way. It notes what happens and what changes need to be made to start again. Sometimes it is called even-mindedness or being nonjudgmental. It is similar to the scientists' ideal of simply noting the facts without leaving any out or adding what is not there. The facts are neither good nor bad. With equanimity we note what is happening without going overboard emotionally. Equanimity is a very important tool to use when we relapse into the old patterns.

We need equanimity to put an end to feeling bad about ourselves. We need it so we can be patient with the reality that effective change is often slow.

Learning to Control Compulsions

If we want to take back control of our minds, then we each need to know what is happening in our minds. We begin by becoming more aware of the events that lead up to the addiction. In effect, we learn to break the habit. Meditation plays a big role in this part. We can use meditation to calm our minds and to learn to keep our minds aware of things we have not wanted to remember. Meditation helps us to have control over our thoughts and the dramatizing that often goes with thoughts and experiences. Meditation is a technique for deepening our concentration so that we can develop wisdom. Some meditations focus more on developing wisdom and others focus more on developing concentration. We meditate so we can have some insight into our minds and our problems, then we begin with investigating some insight developed by wiser people. When we get some understanding, then we spend time just sitting with that insight.

At first the meditations help us to get a grip on our emotions and develop a calmer approach to our problems. Then we use meditation to learn how we fall into our addictive patterns. We learn to undo the habit by becoming aware of it and changing the ways in which we respond to the various triggers for our addiction.

Once we are skillful at identifying and disarming the triggers, we go to the next step: recognizing that intolerance to pain is a big reason for being unable to break the addiction trap. In other words, we learn how to deal with pain, both physical and emotional, as a way of avoiding relapse into the addiction. Meditation can help here as well, especially when it is combined with wisdom. Wisdom just means seeing things for what they really are.

Once we have developed strength in dealing with the pain behind the addiction, we are able to go to the next step. We learn to use our wisdom to develop a more satisfying happiness, particularly that happiness which comes from feeling connected to people, animals, and other living creatures, the environment in general. This can give rise to a sense of our spiritual lives, a sense of connection to complete wisdom and profound compassion.

Addictions and Drug Dependencies

You may have noticed that this definition of addiction does not include the effects of drugs on our bodies. This does not mean that we should ignore the fact that addictions can affect our bodies as well as our minds. If we are caught up in a dependence on things such as tobacco or alcohol or heroin, then we also know that when we try to stop taking the drug, we experience withdrawal symptoms. Withdrawal symptoms make it more difficult to give up the addiction, but they are not the main reason why it is difficult to break the addiction trap.

It is the desperate wanting for more which is the basis of addiction, and wanting comes from the mind. This wanting becomes extreme when the pain of withdrawal becomes stronger simply because the addiction has been our escape from reality and we do not want to face the reality of the pain of withdrawal.

We need to be brutally honest about this. We might need more and more of a drug to get a high, but that does not explain why we needed the drug in the first place and still need it now. People with drug and alcohol addictions have an extra problem. They need to bring their body and brain back to normal and this usually means taking medicine. But even when that happens, if there is no attempt to work on the *mind* of addiction, then it is too easy to fall back into it. We call this relapse.

A Balanced Plan for Undermining and Removing Addictions

Old ways of thinking have not released us from our addictions. We need something new. If we understand habits and how they are formed, we can not only undo those habits, but replace them with new and more effective habits. This book is about retraining ourselves to think and behave differently. There is no magical cure for addiction. It helps if we keep things in perspective and be patient with our progress. Equanimity, of course, is the quality which helps us do just that.

If we look at our addictions with wisdom, then we find new ways of understanding ourselves, our relationships with other people, our environment, and our sense of spirituality. With wisdom, we can see more clearly what we need to do and have hope that our path will lead us there. Wisdom helps us to develop a strong and effective motivation for change, and motivation is one of the most important factors in creating new habits.

If the new ideas are going to be effective, they have to become second nature. They need to become so familiar to us that we do not even have to think about them. We know we can do this because that is the way in which our addictions developed. These ideas are found in each chapter and explain the reasons for the various meditations. The meditations are ways of putting into practice the changes we need to make. Of course we are not actually making the changes when we meditate. Instead we are training our mind to take a different path. These new paths are the beginnings of the new habits we want to replace the habits behind our addictions. The meditations and the thinking parts of the chapters work together to create the motivation and give us the skills we need to make the changes we choose.

This book offers a series of guided meditations that take the reader gradually through each of these steps. Meditation is important because it gives us the opportunity to reflect on new ideas and to take them to heart. When this is done with a positive motivation tuned into wisdom and kindness, then the results can be quite powerful. At the very least, the meditations help us to mentally rehearse the changes in attitude and behavior that we might want to make. This mental rehearsal helps to create positive habits to replace the negative ones of addictions.

We start the retraining with very simple exercises in Chapter 2 and develop our meditation skills gradually with each new meditation. Once we have our emergency strategies functioning, we can take time to understand the mind and how it works. This gives us a sound basis for using habits effectively. Most of us tend to overreact to what is happening around us, especially when that is going to involve pain or loss of some sort. When we know why we do that, we can also undo that overreaction. The only way to know how we overreact is to examine our own minds, which of course means more meditation. The next set of meditations, then, contains ways to become mindful of our experience, in particular to whatever triggers our addiction.

This helps us to move to the next stage: how to manage emotional and physical pain more effectively by making wise choices and using equanimity. We learn to be responsible for our own choices in the ways in which we might manage pain. From that we learn to recognize and forgive the pain we have caused to ourselves and the pain caused to us by others. This step of forgiveness is also a transition from looking inwards to looking outwards. It is the beginning of our reconnecting with people.

When we perceive that people are interfering with what we want, we start to push them away or ignore them. We become isolated, lonely, and disconnected from even the slightest possibility of loving and being loved. There is no point in getting rid of an addiction if it means we have no pleasure, no love, nowhere to call home. We need tools to reconnect. These tools for reconnecting are the simple values that we all know are needed for a satisfying life. As we get more and more trapped into an addiction, we lose sight of these values. When we make an effort to use them again, then we find our lives becoming lighter and freer.

Forgiveness also implies a different set of values—those that create harmony in our relationships. The next stage, then, is to look at the values held by wise people and how these values can restore harmony. As we rehearse these values through meditation and put them into practice in real life, we find that our hearts are not only more loving, but that we are loved in return for our kindness and trustworthiness.

Again, equanimity plays an important role. We learn to direct our equanimity to our own self, which has reacted so badly, and also out towards people who may have harmed us. Equanimity teaches us how to drop the crippling effects of guilt without ignoring the damage we have done. It teaches us how to drop resentment and bitterness towards others without ignoring the damage they may have caused.

Reconnecting is about looking ahead and asking what sort of life we might want when we are free of addiction. Loving and being loved restore meaning into our lives because then we feel connected to all things, including our creative energy and spiritual depth. We reconnect with our spiritual sense in a sane and grounded way. When we lose touch with this inner richness, we feel a very deep sense of uselessness and perhaps a deep feeling of isolation and depression. The great religions teach us how to reconnect with this spiritual depth, which has the nature of profound wisdom and unqualified compassion that we call "compassionate wisdom" in this book. These are the qualities behind a deep and satisfying happiness.

It is important to develop familiarity with the new ideas and ways of acting presented in this book. In this way they become new and positive habits to replace the old negative ones. For this reason, the book offers a series of guided meditations. Each one is designed to help us consolidate the various changes we might want to make. Those of us who are not familiar with meditation could read through Chapter 1, which will help us understand why and how meditation is so helpful. Those of us who do not want to meditate in this way need to find other ways to remind ourselves about changes we want to make. Perhaps we can choose to keep a record of what stands out for us as we read the book, or mark certain pages that are important and read them over and over again.

There are several characters in this book. They are not real people, but like a good novel they are real enough for us to feel the same or to know people who are similar. They have different addictions and different ways of dealing with their addictions. It can be interesting for us to think about what we would do to help any of the characters. It is much easier to do that than to accept what we need to do ourselves! Still, once we see our difficulties in someone else's story, then we can be more understanding about our own needs and possibilities.

The book has also been designed so that it can be used as a manual by self-help or other support groups or as a tool in conjunction with other therapies. It is compatible with other various effective and evidence-based psychotherapeutic approaches as explained in Appendix 1.

Chapter 1 supplies the knowledge basis we need so that we can better understand the various tools and how they work. It describes addiction and explains how meditation can be a powerful method for undoing addictive patterns. The next three chapters take us further into our own minds. We look at the compulsive side of addictive patterns and explore the possibility of changing them by developing equanimity (Chapter 3) and by identifying the things that trigger addictive patterns (Chapter 4). And by taking conscious decisions to make these changes. In Chapters 5 and 6 we look at pain and how addictive patterns are often a way of escaping from physical or mental pain. The meditations in Chapter 6 give alternative ways of dealing with pain.

Once we are free of an addiction, we then need to put into place ways of thinking and behaving which are more effective in bringing happiness into our lives. That process begins by looking at the values we might hold and suggesting other values. In particular, if we remain alone and cut off from loving and being loved, then we will not be happy. This means we also need to investigate the ways in which we can improve our relationships with others. For this reason, the last chapters look at ways in which we can reconnect with people. Chapter 7 is about forgiveness, which arises as we direct equanimity toward our own failings and toward the failings of others. Chapter 8 looks at our relationships with the world around us and the importance of bringing kindness and wisdom into the lives of others in whatever small way we can. Chapter 9 looks at happiness and the meaning of life. After all, if life has no meaning, then why bother trying to get rid of the addiction anyway?

No book can meet the needs of everyone with an addiction. This book offers ideas to heal and strengthen our minds. Perhaps some parts of the book are more relevant to your needs than others. We are all at different stages of breaking the addiction trap. So we each choose what we need and take pleasure and confidence in that choice. While the chapters have a logical progression, there is no harm in jumping to what you feel you need right now.

how we can change the compulsive mind: habits and meditation

1

Irrigators guide the water.
Fletchers shape the arrow shaft.
Carpenters shape the wood.
The wise control themselves.
–BUDDHA[4]

BUDDHISM ASSERTS that the mind can be changed. I doubt whether anyone would dispute that point although we often feel as if we are stuck with an obstinate mind that refuses to do what we want it to. In addictions this feeling of being stuck can be very powerful. But Buddha said that all this can change, no matter how bad it is.

Buddha was a top psychologist. He taught methods for dealing with immediate and urgent situations as well as methods that look into long-term change. For the long term, meditation is an important method. When he was teaching about how to meditate, he suggested a number of tools from which we can benefit. We are going to use three of these tools to help us: mindfulness, introspection, and equanimity. Mindfulness keeps our mind on whatever we have decided to do. Introspection checks whether we are being mindful or not. Equanimity stops the dramatizing and catastrophizing that we get into when we do not get what we want (the craving and grasping that arise from attachment) or we get what we do not want (aversion which gives rise to hatred, jealousy, and depression). These three qualities are not confined to Buddhist practice and are being used successfully in mindfulness integrated cognitive therapy and similar psychological work using mindfulness as a base.

Meditation, though, is not exclusive to Buddhism. You do not have to be religious or spiritual to meditate. It is only a way to train the mind.

In this chapter we move towards the practical tools we need for changing our unwanted habits. First we look at the importance of inspiration. With the hope that arises from inspiration, we find the energy to get on with the slow and sometimes tedious work of changing habits. Then we need to understand how habits are formed. This give us more inspiration when we know that change is possible and there are practical tools we can use to make those changes happen. Undoing the habits, though, requires more than just knowing something about how they got there. To undo these habits we need to find out what we want to put in the place of the destructive habits.

If we are going to meditate, then we need some practical help about how to go about it. This is found in the final third of the chapter. Apart from knowing how to sit, we need to know how to use our mind when meditating. There are three skills we can learn: mindfulness, introspection, and equanimity. Each meditation in this book has a structure that some people might find unusual. This structure is designed to help create and maintain new habits. The last part of this chapter, then, gives practical guidelines for meditating and explains the structure of the meditations.

What Buddhism teaches about the mind and the way in which we make ourselves unhappy is relevant to everyone, not just Buddhists. My hope is that we can find out how to develop our own wisdom and love toward others and ourselves. Wisdom and effective methods guided by compassion form the basis of all psychology and also of sound religious practices and teachings.

Finding Inspiration to Change

Inspiration and hope generate the energy and courage we need to get through the frightening parts of changing our minds. Hope comes from inspiration and also from understanding how the mind works. This leads to faith in the possibility of change. St. Paul in the

Bible talked about faith, hope, and love.[5] If we have faith and hope, then maybe we can also love ourselves enough to see the power of changing to a positive way of life.

There are many ways of finding inspiration. We can read stories about people who have been through the same difficulties. If we know that someone else has been successful in kicking an addiction, then we think we can do this too. Betty Ford, for example, became addicted to drugs and alcohol as a way of coping with the pressures of being the wife of a United States president. She said that she liked alcohol. It made her feel warm. And she loved pills. They took away her tension and her pain. Eventually she was forced into rehabilitation. Later she established the Betty Ford Center for alcohol and drug rehabilitation. Not only did she have the courage to admit that she had problems and do something about them, but also the compassion to help other people with the same problems.

In the twelve steps of Alcoholics Anonymous, alcoholics are advised to rely upon something greater than themselves for inspiration. This greater thing is usually labeled God, though it might be Buddha, Allah, Jehovah, or simply a Higher Power. Whatever the label, the intention is to develop profound wisdom and pure compassion.

Finding Inspiration through Understanding How the Mind Works

If addiction is primarily in the mind, then we need some knowledge of psychology and how it can help us change. Changing the mind does not happen overnight. Just as an athlete needs to train the body over a long period of time and gradually build up strength, in the same way we need to exercise the mind. Meditation is mental exercise.

If we understand the need for mental exercises, then we can be patient toward ourselves. Patience leads us away from guilt. We might have done some stupid and shameful things, but we can change that if we give ourselves time.

The mind is always changing. It is easy to understand that sometimes our mind is cloudy with hopelessness or anger or jealousy.

On other days we feel good. We don't flare up so easily. On those days we are more likely to be helpful to ourselves and helpful to the people in our lives. Imagine what it would be like if we could completely remove all unhappy qualities from the mind. We would be constantly happy. We would be loving. We would be at peace with ourselves and be able to think clearly about any changes that might need to be made to ourselves and to our environment.

The underlying nature of the mind is clean of any negative feelings and any ignorance. In other words, it has the nature of complete compassionate wisdom. By thinking in this way, we can see that the painful parts that cause us so many problems are not essential to our minds. We begin to see the possibility that our minds can be clear and aware. This also gives us hope.

Finding Inspiration through a Meaningful Life

A meaningful life comes from having an effective philosophy about life—from having attitude, preferably good attitude. For example, if my philosophy is "get what I can for myself," then I am going to be unhappy when, through the influence of that attitude, I make life miserable for someone else and then find that I have fewer and fewer friends.

If my philosophy is "nothing matters," then I will become hardened to pain experienced by others. United States soldiers were once given pills to stop them from being fearful on the battlefield. Effectively, the pills were to make them feel that nothing matters other than their job. The pills worked, but the soldiers became immune to the feelings of others, including the people they loved. They become hardened to the pain they inflicted on others, even their families, as well as to the pain they might have experienced.[6]

You might decide to follow your own philosophy or to follow a particular religion. What is important is that this philosophy or religion be based firmly in reality. This reality is not just the material world, but includes the reality of all that is beautiful and courageous and meaningful in our lives, the spiritual reality. A valid spiritual reality always has the two qualities of wisdom and love.

Habits and Change

Realize that the nature of your mind is different from
that of the flesh and bone of your physical body. Your mind
is like a mirror, reflecting everything without discrimination.
If you have understanding-wisdom, you can control the kind
of reflection that you allow into the mirror of your mind.
—LAMA YESHE[7]

Have you ever noticed how we act differently according to what clothes we might be wearing? Wearing a ball gown or a formal suit has a very different feel than wearing shorts and a T-shirt. Wearing dirty, smelly clothes feels different than wearing clean, fresh clothes. The same is true for the way we think. If we are always in a depressed or angry mood, then it may seem as if this is just who we are and there is no hope. When we do these meditations, though, we find that the black moods and thoughts begin to go away, at least while we are doing the meditations. This is evidence that they can in fact change.

Gaining freedom from old patterns gives us the freedom to move toward more effective patterns. First, we become more skillful at recognizing danger situations, the ones that trigger our addictive patterns. Then, we learn tools to use when we are in the middle of these situations. Finally, we practice those tools steadily until, bit by bit, they become habitual. In other words, we are currently trapped by our preconceived ideas and expectations, but by allowing ourselves a little space, we can find and develop new tools for eliminating our addictive patterns and replacing them with more satisfying patterns. To do that, we need to think more deeply about addiction.

Addiction is simply another name for a habit, one which has long-term negative consequences. We have many habits and some of these make our lives much easier by cutting out a lot of extra mental work. These kinds of mental shortcuts make our lives more efficient. They are very practical and valuable.

Because we do not need to think when we are doing something

by habit, it seems as if our actions happen without any control on our side. For example, most of us find it hard to write with the "wrong" hand. We know what our hand ought to do, but it will not cooperate. We have not developed a habit for writing with the other hand, but we can if we decide to.

When we stop to think how a habit is formed in the first place, then we can also see how to change it. It seems that when we learn something, and repeat it often, the thinking part of the brain sends the learned patterns to more primitive parts of the brain where they are stored for long-term use.[8] This process is also called "conditioning." This does not mean that once a habit is formed it is there forever. We can "decondition" these habits. Undoing a habit in this way means replacing the old and unwanted habit with a new, more effective habit. For example, a phobia is a particularly nasty habit. If we have a phobia, then we overreact to whatever triggers the phobia. Someone who has a phobia about spiders could go and live in a place where there are no spiders, but it would be much more effective to learn tools to stop reacting when a spider appears. Similarly, someone addicted to junk food can clean that sort of food out of their kitchen. This does not stop the craving for the junk food, but only access to it. The reason for the craving remains hidden.

Ideas can also be unwanted habits, for example the idea that all bacteria are bad, or the idea that we will always be useless, or bad, or unlovable. Whatever the habit, whatever triggers the habit, undoing the habit begins with changing the way we think. A habit comes from the mind and so replacing the habit means replacing the patterns in the mind. Even very deep habits can be changed.

Motivation, Repetition, and Reward

For change to happen, we use some of the same aspects of mind that created our addiction: *strong motivation, repetition,* and *reward.* We can think of meditation as another habit, but one which has a beneficial effect. As we repeat a meditation over and over again, we will create new habits. When the effects of our new way of doing things kick in, we reward and reinforce our motivation.

Motivation

The most powerful tool for changing old habits is *motivation*. If we do not want to change, then of course no matter how many times we practice the meditations, they will not help. At this stage, our own powerful motivation for following through this book comes from the pain and grief that our addictions have caused. It is the motivation saying "Enough!"

Repetition

The next tool is *repetition* or familiarity. The more frequently we do something, the more likely it is that it will become a habit. That is why athletes train and musicians practice for hours each day. If we want to create positive habits, then we need to put some time and effort into this.

Reward

Even when we do something as simple as choosing to do a meditation, or to apply an emergency tool, we begin to feel a little better about ourselves. Feeling better *rewards* our motivation to create the new habit. We also need to develop some wisdom about pleasure and happiness. We will do that later. Meanwhile we can reward ourselves by giving ourselves a good pat on the back for making the effort to say, "Enough!"

Mindfulness, Introspection, and Equanimity

These are the main mental tools to help us stay balanced as we do any meditation or just when we are thinking about our addictions. Mindfulness helps us to remember what we have chosen to concentrate on. Introspection checks whether we are in fact concentrating in that way. If not, then we use mindfulness to remind us what we are supposed to be doing. Equanimity helps us to keep clear of the catastrophizing mind so we do not freak out at anything that seems bad, or become overexcited at anything that seems good. As we learn to use these three tools when we concentrate, then we are giving ourselves some good strategies for undermining and removing our addiction.

Mindfulness

Mindfulness has the idea of being clear, aware, and steady, not just for a flash, but also for a longer period. By itself it is neither good nor bad. We can be mindful of how to get back at someone who has hurt us, or we can be mindful of our unwillingness to forgive. Revenge does not help us, but watching how we might be stuck on revenge can be very useful. We can be mindful that we are now making a cup of coffee or we can be mindful of our urge for coffee. Either of these can be useful. We can practice our ability to concentrate by being mindful of what we are doing as we make the coffee, or we can be develop more awareness of our addiction to coffee by being mindful of the urges. We can be mindful of our emotions at any moment or be mindful of our sensations at any moment. If we are going to use mindfulness to undermine our addictions, we need to direct it in a positive way.

Mindfulness means staying with whatever we have chosen to be mindful about. When we choose to be mindful, we also choose what we will be mindful about. Mindfulness can help us with our addictions partly because it helps us develop concentration and partly because we reclaim our ability to make choices.

Introspection

Mindfulness is not going be of much use if we do not know whether we are being mindful or not. We need to check. Every now and again we need to take a little step away and observe whether we are being mindful or not. So we try to keep a small part of our awareness ready to check in this way. This is what we mean by introspection. We look inside ourselves to see what we are doing. In meditation this is important so that we know whether we are meditating or whether we have fallen asleep or whether our mind has run away onto something else.

Once we have checked in this way, we can choose what to do next. If we are sleepy, then maybe we need to have some proper sleep, or maybe we have eaten too much, or maybe we are trying to avoid meditating. If our mind has run away, then we can gently bring it back to whatever we are meditating on, or whatever we had decided to be mindful about. Of course, if we are still being mindful, then we just go back to that.

Too much of this observing will interfere with being mindful. So we also need to be balanced in the way we use introspection. When we are great meditators, then we no longer need to use introspection, but for now we are still learning meditation skills and we need the tool of introspection.

Equanimity

To develop effective and positive habits we need another tool which is notably absent from addiction patterns: equanimity. Equanimity is the mind which is not being thrown around when things do not go our own way, and which does not get overexcited when they do. It is a mind which is not grasping on one hand or pushing away what we do not like on the other hand. The same tool is sometimes called "nonjudgmental awareness" or "being in balance."[9]

Equanimity needs mindfulness and introspection if it is to become a powerful tool. If, for example, we make the choice to be aware of any sensations that arise as we meditate, then mindfulness and introspection will help us maintain that awareness. Then as we check our reactions to those sensations, we need mindfulness and awareness and some equanimity, especially if the meditation is becoming uncomfortable. If we then check our emotional reactions, we find that underneath our sensations is the judgment of good or bad. This is where equanimity becomes very important. Equanimity notices that we have made that judgment, but does not make further judgments about whether we are good or bad people. It just notices what has happened.

Using the equanimity tool does not mean that we take no pleasure in our successes or feel disappointment with our failures. It means we do not *overreact* and say things like, "I am useless," "I'll never be able to do this," or "Gee, I'm *so* smart." We use equanimity over and over again in this book.

Some Practical Guidelines for Meditation

Meditation is a specific method for developing concentration. When we are able to concentrate, then we are able to think clearly because our mind is not being distracted. The Buddha gave different meditations to different people according to their needs. He suggested, for example, that concentrating on the breath would slow down a hyped-up mind. TV can help us to switch off our problems because it occupies our minds, but that does not calm us down.

Meditation is a technique for keeping our mind focused in a relaxed and contemplative way. We often fall into a meditative state of mind when we are doing simple, pleasant, repetitive tasks, such as gardening, or surfing (waves, not the net!), playing music, or sitting quietly in front of the fire. In meditation we choose to develop that state of mind and use it to help us change. Sports psychologists use this contemplative imagination when training elite athletes. They ask the athletes to imagine they are racing without making any mistakes or getting flustered by unexpected events. The athletes find that after this mental training, when they start their race they can actually do what they have imagined they would do. Meditation begins with both physical and mental preparations. We prepare our bodies for meditation by finding a quiet, comfortable space and by finding a meditation posture that suits us. We prepare our minds for meditation by choosing a positive motivation and choosing to open our minds to complete compassionate wisdom.

We also prepare our minds by training in mindfulness, introspection, and equanimity.

Most of the meditations in this book present a guided series of reflections. Some of the guidelines help us to keep focused and to know what we are trying to be mindful about. Other guidelines help us prepare our mind and body for the meditation itself, just as an athlete will do warm-up exercises and positive visualizations. The meditations have a beginning, a middle, and an end. The beginning brings our mind into a positive, healing space of wisdom and compassion. The middle is the instruction about what we are trying to do. This gives us a focus for our mindfulness and equanimity and is what most people think of as the meditation itself. At the end of the meditation we remind ourselves about what we were trying to do and enjoy the delight of taking time out. Finally, each meditation closes with a dedication, which affirms our motivation for doing the meditation in the first place. Each of these steps is explained further below.

Meditation puts us into a relaxed but focused state of mind, which can have a strong impact on changing habits. The structure of the meditation brings in the inspiration which can arise when we tune in to wisdom and compassion. We can also use meditation to imagine new and more effective ways of reacting to a situation. When we practice the meditation often, then we strengthen that new way of being. Finally, at the end of the meditation we take our reward, whether a sense of enjoyment or fulfillment or breakthrough or being able to stay with any mental blocks. Meditation, then, is another way of changing habits through inspiration, repetition, and reward.

Physical Preparation for Meditation: Place and Posture

Place

We can meditate anywhere, but it is a lot easier to meditate in some places than others. It helps if we can find a space that is quiet and clean and where we are not likely to be interrupted. If there are other people around, whether they are meditating with us or not, it helps if they are kindly towards us and appreciating our efforts.

If we make an effort to tidy the space and make it look nice, then we are also beginning to tidy our mind in preparation for the meditation. Candles and incense and perhaps pictures or statues can help us to be inspired. We can make our personal space in any way which helps us. If we are preparing a space for a group meditation, then we do whatever will be helpful for that group.

Posture
The most important thing to do when meditating is to keep a straight back, whether you are sitting on the floor, sitting on a chair, or lying in bed.

When we choose to sit on the floor:

- ► We will need a cushion slightly tilted at the back. How big the cushion and how much it is tilted is up to each of us.
- ► We need to experiment to find the best solution. When we are comfortably seated, with our legs crossed as best as we are able, we check that our spine is straight.
- ► Now we tilt our head a little so our eyes would be looking about six feet (two meters) in front of us.
- ► We may each decide to meditate with our eyes open or closed or half-open. We choose the option which suits us best.
- ► We allow our jaw to drop a little but keep our lips gently together.
- ► Next we put the tip of our tongue gently against the top of our mouth near the front.
- ► We rest our hands on our lap, left hand underneath and right hand on top. Alternatively, we can rest our hands on our knees.
- ► Now we check to see that our body is relaxed. When we are in the correct posture, we need very little effort to stay there. We imagine that our body is hanging on our spine and shoulders like clothes on a coat hanger.

When we choose to sit on a chair:
When we sit on a chair, then we need a straight back, but our legs are not crossed. We need a cushion on the chair to make our pelvis tip a little forward so we do not lean against the back of the chair. We need a cushion on the floor if our feet do not touch the floor comfortably. When we do need to support our back, we add a cushion behind us so that it holds our spine straight. Other than that, we settle our spine, arms, and head into meditation posture in exactly the same way as people sitting on the floor.

When we choose to lie in bed:
This is a good option when we are ill and weak. We put pillows behind us so that our spine is as straight as possible, even if we are leaning back. Then we follow the instructions above as much as possible. When you meditate in bed, it is very important that you do not lie in your sleeping position, otherwise you might just fall asleep.

Being sensible
It is important to be sensible about what we can and cannot do when we are meditating. If you have physical problems, then adjust your meditation position to be as close to the instructions as possible. Whatever position you choose, be relaxed but with an alert mind. If pain is distracting you from what you are trying to meditate on, then adjust your position so that you can get back to the meditation. There are meditations in which we investigate what it is like to be in pain. If you are doing that meditation, then you could take the pain of your meditation position as the focus of your meditation.

Mental Preparation for Meditation

Choosing a positive motivation

Any meditation practice is affected by our reasons for doing it in the first place. Someone might be thinking, "I am doing this to escape facing my problems," or "I'm only doing this because I've been pushed into it." These motivations will not put us in the right frame of mind for meditation. What we really need are helpful motivations. This means we think honestly about why we want to do the meditation and how the meditation could help us. At this stage a helpful motivation might be, "I am doing this to stop harming myself and to stop harming others." As we develop wisdom, our motivations will reflect this new way of seeing ourselves.

Useful motivations are those which are in tune with compassionate wisdom. We can then make a deliberate choice to adopt these. There is wisdom in becoming healthy, or calmer, or wiser, or more kind. Harmful motivations come from wanting to protect an unrealistic self-image, or from being greedy or angry. For example, if I am doing the meditation so I can prove what a great meditator I am, then this can protect my unrealistic self-image of being better than everyone else. Before we meditate, then, we check to see where our motivation comes from.

Opening our minds to the inspiration of compassionate wisdom

Meditation is also influenced by the type of mental energy we tune in to. If we tune in to revenge or depression, then we are unlikely to find the meditation useful. There are various positive energies we can tune in to when we meditate, and all these come under the headings of either wisdom or compassion. The meditation becomes a spiritual practice when we decide to tune in to completely pure compassionate wisdom. Some of us may do this through our religious beliefs. Others might do this by recognizing that these two qualities are the main ways of developing good and peaceful relationships with others and with the environment. We each find a way that suits us and we stay with that.

There are many stories of people who have achieved what they want for themselves. These stories give us inspiration to do the same. It makes sense to follow the paths of people who have been successful in escaping their addictions. We can tune in to their energy. There are countless inspiring stories on the internet. For example, one recovered bulimic writes, "My journey to recovery was difficult and I had to take one day after the other. I had setbacks, I had a lot. And every time I fell, I got up again and continued on my journey. I did my best not to look back but forward."[10]

We can also tune in to the inspirational energy of complete freedom, which would be a mind that knows everything and is inescapably kind, the Divine Mind.[11] If we tune in to good energies, we can improve our meditation because we have set our minds in that way. Throughout this book this completely perfected energy is called "compassionate wisdom."

Tuning in to compassionate wisdom also reminds us that we cannot always solve our problems from our own limited inner resources. We need help. In meditation, we can get that help by choosing to tune in to the energies of pure compassionate wisdom.

Closing the Meditation: Looking to the Future

After the meditation itself it is always helpful to take some time to feel the benefits of the meditation and to rest in the energy of pure compassionate wisdom. Then before rising from the meditation it is good to dedicate. This means taking the intention to use the benefit of the meditation for our deeper happiness and the happiness of everyone else. We do this through making a decision for the future. We call that decision the dedication. It will probably be related to the motivation we had for the meditation, and it may also be about ideas which may have come to our mind during the meditation. This is like making a New Year's resolution. For example, you might begin to realize that you are chronically angry. Then your dedication might be to try to observe when you become angry.

Dedications are best kept simple and practical. If your dedication is that you will never become angry again, then you will most likely be quickly discouraged. Instead, try to find a dedication which you can really work with. Freedom from addiction is not just a matter of stopping old patterns. We also need to know what to put in the place of these old patterns. When we do not find other satisfying ways of being ourselves, then we simply replace one addiction with another. So a large part of the journey through this book is about understanding what tools we can use to create a more satisfying way of life.

what can be done right now?

2

Why is it so important to know the nature of our own mind? It's because we all want happiness, enjoyment, peace and satisfaction and these experiences do not come from ice cream but from wisdom and the mind. Therefore we have to understand what the mind is and how it works.
—LAMA YESHE[12]

AN ADDICTION emergency happens when we suddenly find ourselves about to repeat the addictive pattern, or even when we suddenly discover ourselves in the middle of it. We need something to do right at that moment. For example, a smoker might find herself halfway through a cigarette before she even knows she is smoking. Or perhaps a chocolate addict might find himself hovering between taking or leaving the chocolate in the dish. The first emergency solution is to either flee or freeze, both of which are described below. Whichever we choose, we have done something about the immediate situation. That gives us time to do one of the breathing exercises to calm us down. At first we learn to concentrate on the out-breath. Often we hold our breath when we do not know what to do. Concentrating on breathing out will release a lot of that pent-up energy. Then we learn to concentrate on the in-breath. This brings oxygen into our lungs and can relieve anxiety and panic attacks. Later, when we have time, we can do the mental spa baths meditation at the end of the chapter. The mental spa baths combine the in and out movements of breathing and leave us feeling clean and refreshed.

The emergency tools give us a quick alternative to the addictive act. They are not going to stop the craving of addiction but they give us time to make a choice. It is the beginning of taking responsibility. Of course, even if we choose to flee or freeze, if we really want freedom from addiction we need to look at its causes and to cut its roots. That means understanding what brings deep satisfaction instead of the grasping and craving of an addiction.

Emergency Actions: Fleeing or Freezing

When we are addicted, we need help, and we need it immediately, and it needs to work. That is the time for using emergency tools. There are two choices:

Fleeing: We can get out of the situation, escape, until we are able to handle the situation. Sometimes we have to get away from the objects or situations we are addicted to—either by getting rid of them or by going somewhere else. This is the logic behind the teetotal strategy of Alcoholics Anonymous. If there is nothing to tempt us into our addiction, then we stop repeating the addictive pattern. It is not a complete solution for anyone because it does not change the underlying causes of an addiction. Still, it is a good start.

Freezing: We can become like a block of ice and just not react to what is happening until we have time to deal with things more effectively. This means blocking out for a moment or two whatever is happening. We stop everything. This blocking response gives time for the immediate urgency to drain away. A good description of this blocking is "urge-surfing,"[13] which means just riding the wave of desire until it passes. This gives us time to pause and change the compulsive reaction. Like the fleeing strategy, it is a good short-term solution.

Emergency Thought: I Can Change!

The best way to use the emergency tools of fleeing or freezing is to add the emergency thought, "I can change." Simply thinking, "I can change" in itself reminds us that change is possible.

When we use these emergency measures, we can calm down. Even more importantly, when we use them, we have already changed the addictive pattern. We have done something different. We are at the very start of undermining a destructive habit and replacing it with a constructive one. That means that we are able to begin the longer-term solutions.

Breathing and Relaxing Exercises

Once the immediate crisis is over, we can add these breathing and relaxing exercises to help us calm down even more. They are easy to learn and take up little time, but they can be very effective.

First Exercise: The Out-Breath

This is a tool to use when we have, say, thirty seconds so we can improve our ability to relax. We do this by deliberately making a slight difference to the way in which we usually breathe. We concentrate on breathing out.

The body unconsciously relaxes with each out-breath, so in this exercise we deliberately let our bodies relax a little more deeply with the out-breath. It is best to do this when we are at the bottom of that breath, just before we have the urge to breathe in.

Now for the next few moments, as we breathe out, we let our bodies relax. Then when we feel like it, we just let the in-breath happen of its own accord. We only need to do this a few times for it to be successful. As we practice this little relaxation exercise, we can become very skilled at it.

Usually our chest drops down and our ribs become relaxed when we breathe out. We continue to concentrate on each out-breath and discover for ourselves what else relaxes as we breathe out. Where in my body do I feel tension releasing? We each notice what our own body feels like in that pause between breathing out and breathing in.

With a clearer and more relaxed space in our minds, then we can make a better decision about what to do. We can think more clearly about what is happening around us and notice what our mind is doing. Do we really need to be caught in the grasping of our addiction? Do we really need to behave in a destructive way? Do we want to behave differently this time? What do I want to do now?

Second Exercise: The In-Breath

In this exercise, we are trying to be a little more mindful of what our body is doing as we breathe.

We breathe in until our *whole* chest feels tight with air. Some people think that they have filled their chest with air when in fact they have only filled part of the chest, usually the top part. The bottom part also needs to be filled. Filling this part will push the tummy out because the lungs press down toward the abdomen.

Now we hold this breath and count to three. Count quickly if necessary.

Then, we let everything go quickly: both breath and body. We relax everything as fast and as fully as we can. We can make noises as we do this: grunt, or puff. When we are ready, take our next big breath.

- We do this at least three times.
- Now we let our breathing return to whatever it wants to do.
- After our breathing returns to normal, we can repeat the cycle: we breathe in deeply and let the breath go quickly three times and then relax our breathing and our body.

Third Exercise: Breathing and Relaxing

This requires a little more time and concentration because we increase our awareness of our body and what it does as we breathe out.

- First we take a full, but not excessive, in-breath.
- We hold this breath for a short time, enjoying the feeling of fullness.
- Then we breathe out slowly.

We breathe out as we did in the first exercise, noticing how our body relaxes on the out-breath. There is no need to make any effort to force the way in which we are breathing out this time: no need to make it quicker, or to force it to be slow. Each time we breathe out we can let go of more and more tension.

▸ And pause between the in- and out-breath.

We just let it happen the way it wants to, without trying to make it longer or shorter. At the same time, we become aware of how our own body feels relaxed at that brief moment.

▸ Once again, breathe in.

This time as we breathe in we do not try to do anything other than let our body take in whatever air it needs. We do this cycle of breathing a few times, say three times, until we get used to being aware of the cycle of breathing and relaxing.

▸ Now we are ready to relax ourselves even more.

Breathe in and out. As we breathe out, we keep our mind on our own feeling of relaxation that comes with the out-breath and particularly at the end of the out-breath. Each time we breathe out, we try to deepen that feeling of relaxation.

▸ As we breathe in, we let go our mental concentration.
▸ As we breathe out, we deepen the feeling of being relaxed.

We keep doing this as long as each of us wants to. Then we do something quiet: have a bath, listen to music, or sit in a chair for a while . . . whatever you find restful.

How to Use These Exercises When Stressed

If we practice these exercises, even for a few days, we will find that when we are feeling stressed, we can relax with just a few breaths. If we are not feeling stressed, then we are less likely to indulge in our addiction.

Because we have practiced the exercises, we can now connect

breathing out with relaxing. We do this by simply concentrating on breathing out and the pause that follows. No one needs to know what we are doing. You can do this sitting on the toilet, or with your head in a book, or while sitting outside for a few moments.

When we are ready, focus on whatever we need to do next.

Mental Spa Baths

The mental spa bath is another way of relaxing and renewing our minds and our bodies. This is also our first introduction to using meditation. Instead of just doing breathing exercises, we become more aware of the ways in which we can set our minds and the ways in which we can affirm the benefits of meditation as explained in Chapter 1. The meditation below follows this structure. Although the motivation and dedication are given in this meditation, we can always choose our own. Some meditations later in the book suggest we do just that. It is a very simple meditation that can leave our body and mind feeling refreshed.

Meditation 1: Mental Spa Baths for Body and Mind

Motivation

We begin by thinking that by doing this meditation we will feel more alive and more able to deal with whatever comes our way. We think, too, how people around us will benefit by our changed attitude.

Tuning in to pure compassionate wisdom

In this meditation we imagine the energy of inspiration in the form of light, totally pure and radiating light of courage and compassion and deep wisdom surrounding us.

Spa bath for the body

As we breathe in, we feel that the oxygen coming in is carried on light rays of pure compassionate wisdom and taken to every part of our body by our bloodstream. This oxygen together with the inspirational energy of the healing light cleans up any rubbish anywhere in the body. We can focus on any part of our body which is not working properly, just as we might focus on dirty parts of our skin when we shower. We imagine this energy like an inner spa bath that sends tingling bubbles of oxygen through us and through any physical pain.

As we breathe out, the rubbish comes out of our body as carbon dioxide. The carbon dioxide disappears into the atmosphere for recycling.

We repeat this cycle at least three times

Spa bath for the mind

Now as we breathe in, we imagine that the same vibrant light of positive inspirational energy bubbles through every part of our mind, giving us a mental spa bath. We feel it sparkling through all our dark thoughts: any anger, resentment, depression, and so on are washed in this mental spa bath.

As we breathe out, any rubbish in our mind is washed out and totally disappears.

We repeat this cycle at least three times.

Closing the meditation

Rest in this healing light energy of pure compassionate wisdom for a while.

Dedication

Think: "What a precious opportunity I have had, and not only that, I have had this opportunity because I chose to open my mind to positive and inspirational energy. May I achieve this quality quickly and may I have the courage and compassionate wisdom to achieve these goals."

Moving Ahead

When we have become familiar with these exercises, we can choose to use them when we are feeling stressed or anxious or panicky or afraid. We do not need a special place or a lot of time. We do not need to wait until we know more about our addiction. Even if we only get this far, we have made important changes that we can be proud of.

If we really want to get to the basics of our addictive patterns, though, we need to look further into our minds. The next chapter introduces us to the mind and how it works. Addictions are built in the same way as any habit. Any habit can be changed. All we need to do is to replace it with another habit. How we go about doing that is explained in Chapter 3.

freedom from acting compulsively: working with the mind

3

Internal feelings and sensations are aroused whenever you do any activity. When they come up, do not immediately think, "This is good," or "This is bad." Such automatic reactions only generate confusion, obscuring the reality of what is actually happening. Instead, try to be mindful of all these feelings and sensations, and investigate them with introspective wisdom. This will develop in you the habit of alertness, making your mind clearer and less distracted.
—LAMA YESHE[14]

WHATEVER OUR ADDICTION, there is something we are addicted *to*, there is something we *want*. So we think that if we could get rid of the object of our addiction, then we would not be addicted. But that does not always work.

This pulling power does not really come from external things. In fact, the pull comes from our attitude towards these things. We are strongly and compulsively drawn to whatever we are addicted to because we have exaggerated its good qualities. We totally ignore its bad qualities and how it is destroying our lives.

We can discover this for ourselves by checking out how the mind works. What can we do and what can't we do? We do this as we think and check through our meditations. What does our mind actually do? What comes and goes in the mind? What stays in the mind and why? These are questions that we will answer by observing our minds in the next series of meditations on developing awareness and equanimity.

What Is the Mind?

The Buddhist view of the mind is that it has the qualities of being both clear and aware. This is like saying completely pure water has the qualities of two parts of hydrogen combined with one part of oxygen, H_2O. Just as water can be turbulent and polluted but still be water, so too the mind may be turbulent and polluted but still be clear and aware. The impurities of the mind come from intense craving, grasping, and aversion which arise in a mind prone to exaggeration. The activities of the mind, thoughts, feelings, and emotions, are like waves on the water. Just as the waves are made of water but are not an essential quality of water (since the surface of water will be flat if it is not disturbed), so also the working of the mind, although it is mind, is not an essential part of the mind. We know we can get rid of pollution in water and we can let the waves settle. Similarly, we remove pollution of the mind by removing ignorance and developing wisdom. Our mind becomes settled. In this way we can have a mind that is calm and clear and at the same time fully aware of what is happening around us.

We know the mind is always changing. One moment I might be thinking about lunch and another moment I am thinking about what I will write next. I might become distracted by a noise from outside. I might decide to turn on the heater. I might choose to be aware of my thoughts such as wandering into an old pattern like, "I ought to work harder, but I don't so I am bad" without falling into the trap of reacting as if I *am* bad. Since the mind does change, we can take the option to change it to what we want.

I expect you've had the experience of having a song stuck in your head. It really feels as though the music is coming from something other than your own mind, as if you are being controlled by something other than your own thoughts and intentions. In the end, even this changes. The song does not bother you for the rest of your life.

Let's say we have been advised to stop drinking coffee for health reasons and drinking it has been our habit first thing in the morning. At first we go to the coffee machine without even knowing we are there. This time, though, we become aware of what we were about to do and make an herbal tea instead. Yet it feels as though we force ourselves to make the herbal tea because the coffee habit is so strong. Addiction is like that. The addictive habit has become buried in the primitive part of the brain. Our task, then, is to bring it back to the conscious part of the brain, to our awareness.[15]

Neurologists use the word "plasticity" for changeability in the brain itself.[16] Even from this new scientific point of view we can change our minds. We do not have to be stuck in a fixed way of thinking or believing.

Addiction colors our awareness and makes us prone to believing that it can solve our problems. Addictions may relieve pain or dissatisfaction or anger or fear, but they cannot stop that state of mind which led to the addiction in the first place. As Lama Yeshe points out, "In many countries people are afraid of those who act out of the ordinary, such as those who use drugs. They make laws against the use of drugs and set up elaborate customs controls to catch people smuggling them into the country. Examine this more closely. Drug taking doesn't come from the drug itself but from the person's mind. It would be more sensible to be afraid of the psychological attitude—the polluted mind—that makes people take drugs or engage in other self-destructive behavior, but instead, we make a lot of fuss about the drugs themselves, completely ignoring the role of the mind. This, too, is a serious misconception, much worse than the drugs a few people take."[17]

More on Equanimity

Since equanimity is such an important tool, we are going to look further into what it means. Emergency actions and meditations will not heal the pain behind an addiction. Learning to tolerate the ups and downs of life without getting desperate is essential when we are trying to undo addictive patterns. Equanimity can be built up by meditating, just as physical strength can be built up by weight lifting.

Equanimity means looking at things objectively like a scientist should, rather than emotionally. We know that scientists should be objective about their work, because if they are emotional, then they are likely to see things which are not there and miss things which are there. If a scientist badly wants a certain result, he or she is much more likely to make such mistakes. We do the same when we badly want something.

Perhaps you are like Cindy. She has been in and out of a number of relationships and each one of her partners was supposed to be the answer to her dreams. She is addicted to falling in love and imagines she will be truly happy with the next man she meets. She has fallen madly in love again. She is so desperate to have her dream fulfilled that she does not really see her partners for what they are, only for the ways in which they meet her dream. Then she is shocked when she is forced to realize each time that her partners were not what she had thought they were. Eventually Cindy will stop to investigate what this dream is all about. Certainly she wants love, but she has not been very skilled at recognizing it. Learning equanimity will be a big part of her being able to see potential partners in both their good and bad aspects. She will then become less and less desperate for a relationship to prove she is okay. She can begin to choose her partners with more wisdom.

Catastrophizing or dramatizing is the opposite of equanimity. Catastrophizing pain means imagining all sorts of horrible consequences such as being unhappy or in pain. We then get stressed out about it and start to imagine even worse consequences. Let's say I come down with a migraine. I have to take the day off . . . again. Maybe my boss will be angry with me. Maybe I will lose my job. If I lose my job, I lose the house and the respect of my partner and the kids will think I'm hopeless and no one will love me and this all proves I am no good. My migraine has become a catastrophe. I feel much worse than I did before. The worse I feel, the more I catastrophize. Yet, apart from the migraine itself, the rest of my pain comes simply from my overheated imagination. I have lost my sense of equanimity.

Equanimity is not the same thing as dissociating, or cutting ourselves off from feelings and emotions as we do with the fleeing or freezing strategies. Instead we look directly at those experiences and try not to get trapped by them. Instead of compounding any negative feelings with further negative feelings, we simply say to ourselves, "Oh, so that's what's there!" We are looking a little deeper into ourselves and developing a little wisdom.

Equanimity needs help from mindfulness and introspection. Mindfulness means staying with whatever we choose when we think or act or meditate. Introspection means checking whether we are still being aware of whatever we choose to be mindful about. When we check our mindfulness in this way, one of the things we notice is that when we try to concentrate, our mind gets tangled up with thoughts and emotions.

When we find ourselves feeling angry, or needy, or desperately wanting something, or depressed, or jealous, or whatever, then equanimity is the way to step aside from these emotions. That is what equanimity does. It looks at the pain without exaggerating its effects and consequences. It takes a balanced view.

Developing Awareness and Equanimity through Meditation

[Your possessions] are not what's making your life difficult.
You're restless because you are clinging to your possessions
with attachment. Ego and attachment pollute your mind,
making it unclear, ignorant and agitated and preventing the
light of wisdom from growing. The solution to this problem
is meditation.
—LAMA YESHE[18]

If we are going to make changes to our mind, then we need to know what thoughts come and go in our minds. We learn what our senses are doing, our emotions, our reactions to our environment and people and even ourselves. Then we practice having a balanced reaction through applying equanimity.

In the first meditation we investigate our own *internal environment* by becoming aware of *sensations* and how we associate one of the three *feelings* of pleasure, pain, and neutral to those sensations. Then we examine how we exaggerate those feelings into *emotions*. If we can notice the exaggerations, we can use equanimity by training ourselves to see them as they are, for better or for worse. For example, if I am learning to play music, it would be silly to think I was hopeless just because I played one wrong note. If I use the equanimity tool, then I just notice that I've made a mistake and work out what I need to do. As we practice equanimity, we become much calmer because we are not being pushed and pulled by our emotions.

After practicing equanimity towards our internal environment, we look at the way in which we react to our *external environment*. This will also help us in identifying the triggers for our addiction. If I have equanimity towards my environment, I will not get dreadfully upset if, for example, the weather was very hot or very cold. Instead I would accept that this is the way things are on this day and set about doing what I can to make myself more comfortable. And even if I can't do that, if I choose to use the equanimity tool, then I would remain calm.

Next we look at the way in which we react to *people* who are significant to us, for better or worse. What does it mean to apply equanimity here? It means not getting upset if someone does not do what I want. It means not getting overexcited when someone really likes what I am doing (though it is good to take pleasure in being praised). If we can practice equanimity in our relationships, we become much easier to live with. Of course it does not mean that we tolerate bad behavior. Instead, we would be in a better state to see why this person is behaving badly. This meditation also helps us to see how we affect other people through what we believe about them.

After doing all this we can more easily apply equanimity towards our emotions and most importantly to our out-of-balance self-esteem. Now we are in a position to develop *equanimity towards ourselves*. We do that by acknowledging our good and bad points without getting caught into self-loathing or self-glorification.

Meditation 2: Equanimity towards Feelings

Feelings come from the reactions of our physical senses and mental sense. Our senses feel good, bad, or indifferent towards various sensations. When we use the word *feelings* in this book, we are referring to this judgment of pleasure, pain, and neutral sensations. We also have emotional reactions to this awareness of nice, nasty, or neither, but in this meditation we are trying to catch the feeling that we experience with any sensation before the emotions take over. We like the sensation, or dislike it, or don't care either way.

In this meditation we first sit and observe how we react to whatever our different senses are experiencing.

Choosing a positive motivation

Everyone will have their own reasons for doing this meditation. Here we stop and check our own individual motivation. What is my reason for doing this? How will it benefit me? If I benefit from this, how will that benefit others? So think about these questions and choose our motivation as we did for the spa bath meditation.

Here is a suggested motivation: "I am doing this meditation because it is time for me to practice equanimity. If I learn to use the equanimity tool, I will be less likely to overreact to things that do not go the way I want them to. If I do not overreact, then I can deal with the situation more effectively. My life will be easier and I will be a much nicer person to know."

Tuning in to pure compassionate wisdom

Now we make a decision to tune our mind in to pure compassionate wisdom in a way that is meaningful for us. We take a few moments to sense these energies around us. The pure compassionate wisdom energy surrounds us all the time like a gentle breeze on a balmy day.

Next we take a few minutes to be mindful of our breath and nothing else. This will slow our mind down and help us with the meditation.

Feelings arising when using our eyes

We now simply look at different things around us, one at a time. As we look at each one, we check what feelings arise in our mind. Are they nice, nasty, or neither? You may notice a photo of a child. What feelings arise? You may notice a crack in the wall. What feelings arise? You may notice trees outside your window. What feelings arise? Or perhaps there is a brick wall outside your window. What feelings arise?

In this way, one at a time we look at different things around us and check what feelings arise. When we notice a feeling, we do not judge whether or not this is the "right" feeling. We just observe it. This ability to just observe is what is meant by equanimity. At the moment we are just checking on whether we have a reaction of pleasure, pain, or neutrality to this thing we are seeing.

Feelings arising from sounds

This time you might prefer to shut your eyes. It is often easier to hear sound when our eyes are shut. It is sometimes surprising how many sounds there are that we had not noticed before. As we notice a sound, we again check the feelings that arise. Do I like or dislike this sound? Do I just feel indifferent to the sound? We notice how we feel pulled towards the sounds we like and have an aversion to the sounds we don't like. We try to listen to these sounds without this pushing and pulling. This is another way to use the equanimity tool—not being pushed and pulled about by our likes and dislikes. It can be quite a relief!

If you are in a very quiet environment, then you can continue by remembering a sound and remembering the feeling that arose in you at that time. This could be someone's voice, or a car, or the sounds of an accident, or a concert. With these remembered sounds the pushing and pulling of aversion and attachment can be quite strong. Again we try to remember these sounds without the pushing and pulling, that is, with a mind of equanimity.

Feelings that arise with other senses

Now we can do the same with the other three sensations, smell, taste, and touch, one at a time. For example, what is the taste sensation in my mouth at the moment? What feelings arise in connection with this? What taste sensation do I remember and what feelings arose with each one? We take special note of any pushing and pulling that go with exaggerating each sensation. Then we try to recall each sensation without the pushing and pulling effect, with equanimity.

What can I smell? What am I touching? What touches me?

Closing the meditation

We bring back to our mind our personal motivation and reflect on how our meditation has helped us move towards our personal goal. It helps, too, to reflect on how tuning in to pure compassionate wisdom adds to this process. Now we take pleasure, as before, in the fact that we have been able to do the meditation.

Dedication

Here we make a promise to ourselves about something positive we can do in the next few hours or the next few days which will affirm the meditation and bring it into our life. For example we may say, "May the benefits I have received from doing this meditation help to develop some of positive habits I need to replace my addiction. I will try to remember to practice equanimity at least once every day."

Meditation 3: Equanimity towards Our Environment

In this meditation we focus on the outside objects that have come into our awareness. We start our meditation as before by checking our motivation and then taking time to rest in pure compassionate wisdom. Now we become aware of any nonliving object outside our body or mind. We observe it as being just that—a thing. For example, we might become aware of what we are sitting on. It could be a hard or soft surface, but it is just a surface. The object itself is not trying to please or displease us. We note that fact and then become aware of another object, the clothes we are wearing, or a rock, or a flower, and so on.

Each time we observe the object and recognize that it is not trying to please us or make us uncomfortable or angry. In this way we add some wisdom to our equanimity practice. We are also calming our minds so that we are not so thrown by wanting or hating these external things. As we strengthen our minds in this way, we become more able to do the next parts of this equanimity practice—having equanimity towards ourselves and towards other people.

We close the meditation by taking time to reflect on what has been helpful to us and then we dedicate the positive aspects of the meditation.

Meditation 4: Equanimity towards People

This can be more difficult than the previous awareness meditations because people do have intentions towards us. They have their own egos and their own reasons for loving or hating us. People can even change from day to day. One minute we might be a close friend and the next minute be absolutely hated by the same person. It is easy to exaggerate the positive qualities of someone we like. It is just as easy to exaggerate the negative qualities of someone we do not like.

It is even more important in this meditation that we begin and end the meditation with the motivation and dedication. The development of a deep and kind awareness of other people needs lots of compassionate wisdom. Then take time to rest in this energy of pure compassionate wisdom

Before we start the meditation, we make a clear decision about who we might meditate on this time. We develop our ability to concentrate by deciding to stay with just this one person and not let our minds wander to someone else. If, during the meditation, we start thinking about another person, then we stop. We go back to the person we chose to meditate about. We can always repeat the meditation if we want to use other people as our focus.

Motivation and tuning in to pure compassionate wisdom

Once again, we make sure of our motivation. This time the motivation might also include bringing hope and healing into our relationships. Then we focus on our breath for a while to calm our mind. Now we can tune in to the completely perfected compassionate wisdom energy around us.

The meditation

The object of our meditation is this one person we each have chosen. We think about the different experiences we have had with this person and especially the ways in which we pull this person towards us when we need her or him and push that person away when we do not like her or him.

Think: "This pushing and pulling come from my side. These attractions and aversions come from me and the ways in which I overreact. Even though this person may sometimes be kind to me and sometimes hurt me, the wanting and the rejection come from my side, from my own mind. How would this person appear to me if I was not constantly being thrown around by my tendency to exaggerate his or her good and bad qualities? What qualities would I see if I dropped my exaggerations and used a mind of compassionate wisdom instead?"

Closing the meditation

Now we take time to contemplate how this meditation has affected us. We remember that any positive effects arise from wisdom and compassion. If you cannot find answers, don't worry. This meditation is not easy and it is not likely to have instant results. Even if the only thing you have achieved is to be quiet for a while, then be happy about that.

Dedication

Here is another suggestion for a dedication: "I will try to use the positive aspects of this meditation to continue on my path to breaking out of addictive patterns and to developing my own compassionate wisdom energy."

Meditation 5: Equanimity towards Ourselves

This is probably the hardest of all the equanimity meditations. This is when we extend compassionate wisdom to ourselves: our good self and our bad self. These good and bad selves have arisen through exaggeration. If we exaggerate a positive quality, we then have to defend that exaggeration against any negative characteristic that seems to threaten it. We tend to do that by pushing the bad characteristics out of our mental sight.

Carl Jung described how we divide ourselves into two parts, "ego" (the parts of ourselves we admire) and "shadow" (the parts of ourselves we loathe). This comes about because we do not look at ourselves in an unbiased way. We become addicted to some parts of our personality and despise other parts. This creates an inner dissatisfaction. The more we try to maintain the ego, the stronger the shadow becomes. Often we make this worse by thinking about ourselves in a fixed way that allows no possibility of change. This addiction to our own self is a much more subtle addiction than the obvious addictions such as drugs and alcohol. We flip between being inordinately proud of ourselves and despising ourselves. This is painful. It causes our relationships to be painful. After all, how can anyone relate to us if we are swinging between self-loathing and unrealistic self-pride?

The object of meditation this time is emotion. In other words, we specifically focus on the emotions that arise from our feelings of good, bad, and indifferent. In the first of the equanimity meditations, we made the choice to *not* follow up these emotions. This time we make the choice to meditate on them. We might choose to meditate on sensations and feelings that arise in our immediate, present environment. We might also choose to meditate on an event or person that sets off strong sensations, feelings, and emotions.

Let's say you choose to base your meditation on an event such as a family argument. This time you contemplate an aspect of that event and try to disentangle the sensations, feelings, and emotions. Sensations are what you feel with your body. Feelings assess whether that sensation is nice, nasty, or neutral. What emotions arise as a result of those sensations and feelings?

As we now know, equanimity means not getting caught in further exaggerations: "Oh, I am so bad because this is what I did," "Look how good I am," "How could anyone love someone like me?" and so on. In this next meditation, equanimity means not judging whether we are good or bad people, but just noting what happened.

It is best if we go through one event at a time, or even just one aspect of an event. Each of us makes our own choice of what to meditate on. Later we can change to another event. We stay with what we have chosen for as long as we can before going on to another event.

We need to remember to start our meditation by checking our motivation and then resting in the energy of pure compassionate wisdom to help us with the meditation. We can also make a deliberate decision from our own side to try to keep our minds on the meditation and not start thinking about other things or falling asleep. Decisions like that help with our concentration. Then we always finish by resting in feeling satisfied with any small gains we might have made, and dedicate by recalling any decisions we might have made.

The meditation

We begin by making a list of those aspects of our own selves that we despise: our loathed self. This is that part of our self that undermines us and steals our self-esteem. We give our loathed self a name and a personality. Most of us can recognize and feel aversion to this part of us.

Now we make a list of those aspects of our own selves that we admire (at least on a good day): our proud self. We give this glorified self a name and a personality. We can recognize and feel our exaggerated attraction. Think how much we all would like to be just the proud self and nothing else.

Then we make a list of some aspects of our selves which are neither despicable nor admirable: the neutral self. We give this neutral self a name and a personality. We easily recognize our indifference. We neither care about this part of ourselves nor despise it.

We now find how to send loving-kindness and compassion to these three aspects of ourselves.

The motivation
Generate strongly the wish, the prayer, that each of these aspects of oneself in turn be free: firstly focus on the loathed self, then the proud self, then your neutral self.

Tuning in to pure compassionate wisdom
Take time to be aware that you are surrounded by the incredible energy of wise loving-kindness that has various names.

The visualization
We take the loathed self, prideful self, and neutral self, one by one, and generate loving-kindness and compassion towards each one in turn, beginning with the loathed self.

Think strongly:

"May this loathed self (prideful self, neutral self) be free of the hurt, the anger, the grasping, the arrogance, the jealousy, and all such mental afflictions.

"May this loathed self (prideful self, neutral self) be free from the suffering that arises from such afflictions.

"May this loathed self (prideful self, neutral self) recognize and cultivate loving-kindness and compassion, patience and generosity, and all other wholesome qualities.

"May this loathed self (prideful self, neutral self) experience the sense of well-being, of joy and bliss, of calmness and clarity which arise as the positive qualities flourish.

"May this loathed self (prideful self, neutral self) develop the profound quietness of mind that allows me to develop great compassion and deep insight.

"In this way, may this loathed self (prideful self, neutral self) be well and happy.

"May this loathed self (prideful self, neutral self) be a source of similar peace and joy and well-being to all those people whom I love and, indeed, all people and creatures with whom I have contact, and even those people and creatures I have never met."

Imagine these things to be so now, as realistically as you can. Imagine it to be so right now.

Closing the meditation

Take some time to feel what it is like to have equanimity towards yourself. Think, too, about all the people that have helped you come to this point and how fortunate you are to have this opportunity to see yourself without being judgmental.

Dedication

Here is another example of a dedication:

"In doing this meditation, I have tried to make a small change in my mind. This small change in my mind will help me to change my life for the better. I have done my best to do the meditation. It was not perfect, but that is okay. I will be patient and remember that training the mind takes time.

"I set out to meditate today so that I can develop more compassionate wisdom. Let me take a moment to reflect on the benefits I have received.

"May my compassionate wisdom continue to grow. May I never lose the compassionate wisdom which I have found. May I find even more wisdom nuggets and even more compassion.

"May the positive energy I have generated radiate and create the space for compassionate wisdom to grow in the minds and hearts of other people: my family and friends, anyone who has problems similar to mine, in fact to any living creature whatsoever. May they also develop complete wisdom and profound compassion. In this way, may my inner peace become a contributor to world peace."

Myths and Realities about Happiness and Pleasure

We often experience a desperate wanting and desperate aversion towards ourselves, towards our addictive patterns, and towards the object of our addiction. This comes about from a common and basic misunderstanding about the differences between happiness and pleasure. Pleasure comes from our senses when the contact with some object feels good. It is not the feeling good which is the problem, but wanting to hang on to that feeling. We become unhappy when we have no access to that nice feeling. If we have access to whatever give us pleasure, then we grasp it and try to hang on to it. The more we want it, the more grimly we try to hang on to it. Unfortunately, however grimly we hang on, what we want does not and cannot last forever. Buddha understood this. He called it the suffering of change. What he meant was that what seems to be happiness is already, from its very first moment, affected by the fact that the object bringing this pleasure will eventually change. In addition, our own bodies and minds are constantly changing. This is called impermanence.

Imagine, for a moment, that you are on the beach on a hot day. The water is so inviting that you can hardly wait to drop your towel and run into it and cool down. What pleasure, then, will come from swimming or soaking in that cool liquid. It feels as if this pleasure will last forever. But the reality is that after a while you begin to feel waterlogged. The water is no longer inviting. Now it is your towel that is going to give you pleasure. Fine. But after a while, you get hot again. Then the water is so inviting once more . . . until you feel waterlogged, and so on. Mostly we do not get emotional about the fact that on a hot day at the beach we are likely to enjoy getting into the water when hot and out of the water when cold. We can accept the changes.

What happens, then, if you decide to go to the beach on a hot day and, after an hour, an unexpected cold, rainy change blows up turning the glassy waves into a gray, choppy mess and soaking your towel in the bargain? Suddenly the pleasure of being on the beach has gone. How will you react? If you desperately wanted a typical beach day, then you are likely to be angry. The more you wanted the beach day, the more upset you are likely to be. You are angry because what you thought would last has not lasted. It was impermanent. What is reality: the dream of a perfect beach day or the changing of that perfect day into something else? Whatever our pleasures may be, they are subject to change. There is really not much point in getting upset.

Addiction is about wanting happiness, but the happiness that comes with addiction is necessarily a temporary, impermanent pleasure. We get trapped into addiction because we want this apparent happiness forever. We cannot have it forever and yet we still yearn for a lasting happiness. What does this mean? Is it possible to find a lasting happiness? We will leave that question to later chapters.

Making the Most of Pleasure

It is not wrong to be happy and appreciate the pleasures of life. The secret is to enjoy these things while we have them and not to be resentful when they naturally pass. We can set up our lives so that happiness and pleasure are more likely. For example, keeping the house reasonably clean and neat means we enjoy it more often. We will enjoy it even more when we do not get upset when the house naturally becomes untidy and dusty again.

Making the most of pleasure means having equanimity towards that as well. If we give ourselves time to practice equanimity, then we find that we become more aware of what we are thinking and how we are reacting to our inner and outer worlds. This gives us a basis for identifying the triggers which throw us into the compulsiveness of addiction. If we can identify the triggers, then we have much more power to undo the negative, compulsive patterns and to replace these with something else.

finding triggers
and choosing to change

4

The mental pollution of misconceptions is far more dangerous than drugs. Wrong ideas and faulty practice get deeply rooted in your mind, build up during your life, and accompany your mind into the next one. That is much more dangerous than some physical substance.
—LAMA YESHE[19]

THE TRIGGERS for our addictions are those things or thoughts that set off an automatic reaction so that we find ourselves in our addictive pattern without knowing how we even got there. The triggers might be external or internal or both. An external event such as a song can set off an internal trigger such as loneliness. We may not be aware that we heard the song, but just that the feeling of loneliness has welled up again and we want to escape it. We may not be aware of the loneliness, but just the thought of wanting to fix some dissatisfaction. We may not be aware of the dissatisfaction, but just of taking or doing whatever will ease it. We may not be aware of what we do, but suddenly discover we are in the middle of our addiction. If we can identify the trigger, then we can disarm its effect and we are no longer caught in that particular compulsion.

If you want to find the triggers for your addiction, you need time to sit and contemplate. There are some triggers which you might have in common with someone else with a similar addiction. For example, cigarette addiction can be triggered by the smell of tobacco smoke, or the sight of a cigarette. There are other triggers which are unique to you. For example, you might find that a certain perfume will trigger feelings of anger because someone who hurt you wore that perfume. Then the smell triggers the impulse to take up the cigarette to try to calm the anger.

As we identify the immediate triggers and learn to recognize them, then we often find that there are other more subtle triggers. Sometimes people feel that if they discover another trigger, then that means that what they did before was wrong or a waste of time. Don't get caught in that trap. We usually have more than one trigger to any addiction. If you find other triggers, this probably means you are doing good work in opening your addiction trap.

How Does Something Come to Be a Trigger? Emotions and Habits

Through the process of familiarity we learn to see things in a certain way and ignore other things which do not fit in. We develop habits. As we have seen, habits can be a very useful process, but they can also be a barrier to learning new things. Imagine a tennis coach trying to improve the way in which you serve the ball. At first it is very hard to do this new way of serving because the older habit, even though it is less effective, has made a deep imprint. If we want to improve our tennis, then we need to practice and practice the new way of serving. In other words, we need to develop familiarity with the new way until it has become a new habit. We first need to catch ourselves at the moment just before we fall into the ineffective pattern. If we can catch that moment, the trigger, then it is much easier to learn to undo the whole pattern. Next we can undo the power of familiarity and habit first by recognizing it and then by using our mind, particularly our imagination, to create a different and more useful familiarity

We can also have associations to good events because we like the experience and do not want to mask the emotion that comes with the memory. Do you have a special music track that reminds you of something good? The track was probably playing in the background at that special event. We enjoy bringing our memories back by playing the track again and there is no good reason to change that habit. For another person, the same music can be associated with the breaking of a relationship and trigger unhappy emotions. The same track can be associated with either good or bad memories.

External Triggers

Any external thing can trigger your addiction. It could be a particular advertisement, a smell, seeing someone else indulging, oppressive weather, an untidy bedroom, children crying or squabbling, your boss (or partner, or parent) threatening or ignoring you, and so on. There are so many possibilities that we each have to work out our own triggers.

Sometimes the association happens due to a very strong, stressful emotion. If you were badly hurt in a car accident, then perhaps the smell of burning rubber brings it all back to you, or the sight of blood, or a loud bang. You smell or see or hear these things and the terror floods back and you need relief from that terror.

Sometimes the trigger has become associated with an addiction because it is in the background, like the music track mentioned above. This is association through familiarity. Maybe you know someone like Duncan. He has an addiction to gambling and always goes to the casino by car. Every time Duncan goes to the casino, he has to pick up his car keys. After a while, just picking up the car keys is enough for him to think about gambling. Picking up the car keys has become a trigger for his gambling just because it has happened so many times. Duncan could be addicted to anything that requires him to jump into his car and the car keys would trigger that addictive pattern. We will find out more about Duncan's addictive patterns in Chapter 5.

We can take these triggers one step further. Take Abby. She has a shopping addiction and she sees an ad about a sale at her local shopping center. The ad is an obvious trigger for that addiction. Now imagine that she has developed this addiction to compensate for feeling like a nobody. She has been bullied at school, so when she sees the bullies with their backs to her, she thinks they are talking about her. How will she cheer herself up? Probably by doing even more shopping. The ad and the group of people with their backs turned are external triggers. The feeling of being nobody is an internal trigger.

How is Abby going to find out about the triggers for her shopping addiction? Only by investigating her own mind and finding what is there. This is what we are about to do.

Internal Triggers

An internal trigger is something within our own body or our own mind which sets off the addiction trap. It can be a physical sensation in any part of our bodies, inside or out. For example, it could be . . .

A feeling of being too hot or too cold
Sensitivity in some part of your body such as lips or fingers
Tightness in throat or shoulders or thighs or somewhere else
An upset stomach
Heart palpitations
. . . and so on.

The other internal triggers are our emotions and thoughts, in other words, things going on inside our mind. We might be feeling angry, or jealous, or depressed, or hyped-up or some other uncomfortable emotion. Positive emotions are enough by themselves. They do not trigger us into addictions because they are, by definition, pleasant and do not harm ourselves or others. Thoughts which can be triggers might be . . .

I'm not good enough
No one loves me
I'm all alone
I'm trapped in a bad relationship
I'm different and people laugh/stare/make fun of me
My life is out of control
I'll be out of the in-group if I don't smoke/drink/eat/behave the way they do
I can't put up with my bad feelings/pain any more
. . . and anything else you might add.

Some negative thoughts lead into addiction because we can't find another way around a dilemma such as:

I have to calm myself down, or else . . .

I have to zap myself up, or else . . .

I can't help this because my father/mother/family member is the same and so it must be genetic

. . . we can each add our own negative thoughts.

Disarming the Addiction Trigger

If there are no bullets in the gun, then even if you pull the trigger there will be no harm. The bullets, in this case, are ways in which we react to the different triggers. The finger that pulls the trigger is an unconscious thought or habit. We begin by uncovering the triggers and then we have the possibility of unlocking the automatic reaction.

Undoing the Automatic Reaction

Later we will meet Jake. He has an addiction to chocolate and junk food. He discovers, through doing the first meditations below, that one trigger for his addiction is a cup of tea. In other words, whenever he has a cup of tea, he automatically has a piece of chocolate at the same time. The chocolate is kept near the tea tin. While he is waiting for the kettle to boil, he takes the chocolate and eats it before he even knows what he is doing.

As Jake does the meditation below, he disarms the cup of tea as a trigger for his addiction. He begins with imagining he is *about* to have a cup of tea. Then he imagines himself going to the shelf where the tea and chocolate are kept. But this time in his imagination, he is not going to take the chocolate. He chooses a simple alternative action. He visualizes himself putting the chocolate out of sight before he makes his cup of tea.

The more often he does this visualization, the more likely it is that he will actually put the chocolate away. What will probably happen at first is that his unconscious mind will get confused because it now has two habits associated with making tea: the old habit and the new one created by his imagination. This confusion then makes him pause and think about what he really wants to do: to take the chocolate or not take it. At first he might even defy this impulse to be different. If he does, he will probably feel bad about that, but this time there is a big difference. He has *consciously* chosen to eat the chocolate instead of eating it compulsively and automatically. Even a bad choice is still a choice. The important thing is that he can now make a choice, whether good or bad, whereas before he reacted automatically.

Meditation 6: Finding the Triggers

This meditation focuses on what has happened just before we indulged in our addiction so we can identify the immediate trigger. The next meditation will help you to find the triggers behind the immediate triggers: the subtle triggers.

Motivation and tuning in

Begin your meditation by thinking about how your addiction has harmed yourself and perhaps harmed others. Think strongly that you would like to stop creating harm in this way.

Think that your motivation is firstly to clear away obstacles from your mind that stop you from thinking clearly and secondly to fill your mind with love and wisdom. Now tune in to the energy of pure compassionate wisdom, feeling that you are being nurtured by this energy.

The meditation

Slow your mind down by just being aware of your breathing for a few minutes.

Now bring into your mind a recent time when you indulged in your addiction. Take your mind to the point where you just started. Now go back a fraction of time to the point where you are just about to start. This is the moment we will meditate on.

Focus on this moment when you are just about to start.

External triggers

Try to build up a vivid awareness of your surroundings at that time. Imagine this past event as a present experience. Where are you? Are there people around or are you alone? What can you see? What smells are there? What taste is in your mouth and what sounds can you hear? Is your body aching, or numb? Are you comfortable or uncomfortable?

Any of these might be an external trigger. View the trigger with a mind of equanimity. Stay with your awareness of this for as long as you can.

Internal triggers

Now build up a vivid awareness of what was happening in your mind at that time. Did you have any pain? Were you stressed? Were you winding down? Were you winding up? Had you just had a fight? Were you lonely? Had someone disappointed you or had you disappointed yourself? Was there someone or some people you were trying to impress? Did you feel cheated by life? Were you unable to cope? What else?

Any of these might be internal triggers. View these with a mind of equanimity.

Stay with your awareness of this moment as long as you can. See that moment as vividly as you can. Plant firmly in your mind those aspects of that moment which were triggers that set you off into the addiction.

Acknowledge to yourself that this is your reality, and addiction is, or has been, the way in which you cope with your reality.

Closing the meditation

Once again, allow yourself to abide in the energy of pure compassionate wisdom. Imagine this energy being absorbed into your body and healing all hurt and pain and sickness. Allow your body to feel relaxed, at ease. Imagine this energy of pure compassionate wisdom being absorbed into every part of your mind, healing all negative emotions and leaving your mind peaceful and calm.

Rest in that state as long as you can.

Dedication

Take pleasure in what you have achieved in this meditation, even if parts of it were painful to remember. Now make a conscious choice that you will use the energy that comes from this pleasure to continue to make positive changes to your life.

Further work on finding the triggers

This meditation needs to be repeated often if you want to get a better feeling for the addiction triggers. As you become more aware of the moments before you fall into your addictive pattern, you can more easily change the pattern

As you repeat the meditation, you can take it back to the time before the moment before the addiction, then a fraction earlier, and earlier, and so on. As we do this, we gain more power to protect ourselves from the compulsiveness of an addictive pattern. We keep uncovering levels of dissatisfaction and pain. Having done that, then we can start to try other ways of dealing with dissatisfaction and pain.

Freedom to Choose

Freedom to choose is also freedom to create a positive motivation. Why do I want to stop eating chocolate? For my health? To prove a point? To please someone? To lose weight? Any of these motivations will help me, but the one that helps most is the one with greatest wisdom behind it. For a person who has felt overwhelmed by others, wisdom may be the determination to stand up and prove a point. Wisdom for the bully may be to stop and really listen to what others are saying.

Freedom to choose does not necessarily mean that we will be immediately successful in actually making the changes. Giving into our addictions does not necessarily mean we are weak. Sometimes our motivations are hidden from us. I might think I want to stop eating chocolate so I can lose weight, but perhaps I am fooling myself. Maybe I am self-medicating for physical pain or stress. Maybe I want the warmth of human love. Maybe I am being driven by low glucose levels. Maybe I have become a diabetic. It may just mean that I have still not discovered what the addiction is trying to replace. There is no point in feeling bad about that and then giving up. Instead we simply continue tracking down the reasons behind our own addictive patterns.

Everything in this book is about making choices. Some choices are easier than others, and what one person finds easy will be hard for someone else. When we realize that we can make choices, then we also begin to feel better about ourselves.

Meditation 7: Choosing to Change

Once we know what the triggers are, we can use our new awareness to change our behavior when the triggers are around. This time we are deliberately trying to develop a different and positive habit in place of the addictive habit. It is up to each of us to develop this meditation. We need to work out what would be a wiser response to the trigger, and it needs to be something realistic. It has to be something we can actually do at that moment. We need to be strictly honest at this point. Once we each decide what is appropriate, then we imagine that we go ahead and do just that. The more we imagine this new pattern happening, the more likely it is that we will change our addictive pattern. I know someone who was able to serve a tennis ball the first time he picked up a racquet. When asked how he could do this, he said that he had watched it on TV. I suspect he did not just watch it, but imagined himself there playing tennis like the professionals.

Motivation

Begin your meditation by thinking about how your addiction has harmed yourself and perhaps harmed others. Think strongly that we would like to stop creating harm in this way.

Now we feel that we are surrounded by loving-kindness and compassion and wisdom and that this energy is readily available to us. Our motivation for this meditation is firstly to clear away obstacles from our mind that stop us from thinking clearly and secondly to fill our mind with love and wisdom.

Tuning in to pure compassionate wisdom

We slow our minds down by just being aware of our breathing for a few minutes. Then we think how our own mind, if it could be completely pure, would be supreme compassionate wisdom energy. We feel that this purified energy is guiding our meditation.

The meditation

Now we each bring into our mind a recent time when we indulged in our addiction. We each take our mind to the point where we had just started.

From that first moment we take our imagination forward in time, imagining this as vividly as we can. This time, instead of unwittingly falling into our addiction, we make a conscious choice to do something else. For example, imagine that instead of picking up the cigarette, or ordering the beer, or clicking online, or going shopping or . . . imagine that instead of that, you consciously decide not to do that thing and you consciously decide to do something else.

Now we meditate on the outcome of doing things differently. Here is a pattern we can follow, imagining each step as vividly as we can:

- ▸ Imagine your first moment of awareness of the trigger.
- ▸ Imagine yourself stopping the usual actions that lead into your addictive patterns.
- ▸ Imagine yourself doing something positive and helpful instead of going into your addictive pattern.
- ▸ Imagine the outcome of putting this new pattern into practice and what changes happen as a result.

Repeat these steps in your imagination so that your mind begins to create a new habit.

Closing the meditation

As before, allow yourself to rest in the energy of pure compassionate wisdom, this time in the form of healing light. Imagine this light being absorbed into your body and healing all hurt and pain and sickness and replacing it with inner strength and courage. Allow your body to feel relaxed, at ease. Imagine the light of pure compassionate wisdom being absorbed into every part of your mind, giving you the power to really do what you have imagined yourself doing.

Rest in that state as long as you can.

Dedication

Take pleasure in what you have achieved in this meditation. Now make a conscious choice that you will use the energy that comes from this pleasure to continue to make positive changes to your life.

Exaggeration and Pain

As we begin to find the triggers and increase our practice of mindfulness and equanimity, we begin to see that the triggers are associated with badly wanting something or desperately avoiding something.

Nobody wants to be in pain. It causes all sorts of limitations which are frustrating and sometimes frightening. We can often deal with short-term pain by clenching our teeth and getting on with what we have to do. This does not work in the long term. Chronic pain needs different solutions. This is true for both physical pain and the emotional pains which come from the negative states such as anger, jealousy, depression, and greed. Addiction itself is like a chronic pain, but also addictions help us to mask chronic pains. We have already started to investigate the underlying dissatisfaction and pain behind our addictions. In Chapter 6 we are going to find tools to help us with the pain itself. First we will take a closer look at how we create pain for ourselves when we are trapped by any intense pulling towards us of the things we want and pushing away of the things we do not want.

exaggeration, denial, and pain

5

After all, the Buddha wanted us to have as much perfect pleasure
as possible; he certainly didn't want us to be miserable, confused or
dissatisfied. Therefore we should understand that we meditate in order to
gain profound pleasure, not to beat ourselves up or to experience pain.
If entering the Buddhist path brings you nothing but fear and guilt
then it's certainly not worth the effort.
—LAMA YESHE[20]

IF ADDICTIVE PATTERNS come about because we do not want to
feel dissatisfaction and pain, then we need to find better ways of
managing pain. First we need to find out how much of the pain is
physical and how much is emotional or psychological. If we have
been hurt in a car accident, then most of the pain is probably physical. On the other hand, if the wind blows over my expensive vase,
then the pain I experience is mostly psychological. If someone who
hates me throws a brick at me, then I am likely to experience both
physical pain as a result of the bruising of my head, and psychological pain as a result of bruising my ego.

Learning to manage either physical or psychological pain is
very important. Not only do we need something better than an
addiction to manage pain, but we also have to deal with the pain
that arises when we decide to say "Enough!" to the addiction. We
understand that withdrawal from drug and alcohol addictions is
physically painful. It is important to also understand the emotional
pain that can arise when we withdraw, whether our addiction has
been drug-related or not.

Let's return to our typical shopaholic, Abby. Abby is feeling better because she has now definitely decided to break her habit. Unfortunately next time she goes shopping, she ends up splurging on her credit card again. What has gone wrong? In her case, she saw the school bullies again. She assumed they were talking about her. Once again, she feels isolated and frightened. Abby needed something to give her comfort and for her that is shopping. Other shopaholics might think, "If I don't look good, I won't feel good" or may just be bored or jealous. The illogical thinking goes like this: "Without shopping, there is no way to feel happy because shopping is the only way to feel happy." Behind such thoughts is often emotional pain such as feeling unloved and unlovable, or feeling totally disconnected from the rest of the human race, or the grief of having our connections torn through such things as injury, illness, and death. In Abby's case her appearance was constantly criticized by her older brother and his friends. No wonder she always felt that people were talking about her.

Abby is very enthusiastic to change, but it will take time.

Loaded Emotions and Exaggerations

As we have already learned, our inner feelings and emotions come about from the ways in which our minds react to what is happening in our life. As we already know, feelings themselves, such as liking or disliking or feeling neutral about something, come when we become aware of physical or mental sensations. Emotions come after the feelings. So emotions on the negative side can be anger, greed, pride, jealousy, feeling worthless, revenge, and so on. On the positive side the emotions can be love, joy, peace, happiness, satisfaction, confidence, inner strength, delight, and so on.

In other words, feelings are not the problem. The problem comes in the way we *react* to those feelings and sensations and exaggerate them with unbalanced emotions.

Emotional pain or pleasure comes *after* we experience the feelings of nasty or nice. Emotions happen when we get caught up in the feelings and begin to see or imagine consequences of these feelings and we have some sort of inner investment in what is happening. We badly want something or we desperately want to avoid something. We want inner things such as love and praise. We want outer things like money, or a comfortable bed, or the best food, or cool drinks on a hot day. We stress when we do not have them. We invest in such things because we think they will bring about happiness.

This does not mean we should not have any wants. Some things are indeed important, such as having enough food to stop us from being hungry, or having people around who are kind to us. We invest a lot of energy in trying to have what we think is important. It is not the investment of energy itself that is the problem, but whether this energy comes from a wise mind or from an unclear mind. If I invest my energy unwisely, say, in getting an expensive sports car (because that would show everyone how good I am), then I probably would get upset if I could not get that car, or someone scratched it, or someone abused me because of my wealth. A wise investment in a car would be something like, "I need it because there is no local transportation." Then it would not matter much what sort of car it was as long as it did the job. An unwise investment of energy leads to a lot of unhappiness.

Let's take a deeper look at Duncan, our gambling addict. We all know someone like him. He is not a very nice person to know, but as we look at his story, then we start to see how he makes life worse for himself and how we, too, go for our addictions when life goes bad. Be kind to him, though. Then it might be easier to be kind to yourself. We all need kindness if we are going to break away from our own addictive patterns. Like each of us, Duncan is masking his own pain. He needs a better solution than his addiction.

Duncan is a middle manager in his firm, overweight and unpopular. At the moment he is annoyed because an e-mail he wanted has not arrived. One of the factors behind this annoyance is his expectation that the e-mail should arrive today, but the expectation has fallen flat. The e-mail did not arrive. Now his mind begins to worry about the consequences. Maybe it means that he is unloved, unwanted, unappreciated by his superiors, which then means that he is no good and he feels bad about himself for being no good. Some very uncomfortable emotions are agitating him. He exaggerates around the fact that the e-mail is missing and begins to imagine dire consequences. If Duncan had learned something about equanimity, then maybe the outcome of the missing e-mail would be simply that he would be unable to do what he wanted to do. He might be mildly annoyed instead of being agitated.

It is not the event itself which is the main problem. Whether there is or is not something in his in-box does not normally upset him. The computer is not trying to make him upset. The person who should have sent the e-mail may not be deliberately inconveniencing or ignoring him. Let's say another e-mail doesn't arrive that day, but one that did not matter to him one way or the other. Duncan does not get upset. There is no reason for him to get upset by what appears or does not appear on his computer screen. What makes him upset is his own emotional exaggerating about the first missing e-mail. For Duncan, the one missing e-mail implies he is not appreciated by his superiors. The other missing e-mail is of no consequence. Like us, when an emotion becomes exaggerated, Duncan gets angry, or depressed or upset in some way.

We can see that Duncan's emotional response is not really related to the first missing e-mail, but maybe to how Duncan sees his relationship with the person who was to write the e-mail and almost certainly to how he feels about himself when he is not appreciated. His shaky self-esteem has created a strong grasping for a certain result. Underneath he secretly feels bad about himself and this e-mail is supposed to stop him from feeling bad. Unfortunately neither the computer nor the sender knew about this.

Something which started out as a sensible desire, expecting a particular e-mail, has now transformed into a major problem and sent Duncan into his addiction trap. He is feeling bad and he hates being like that. He rings up the betting agency to distract himself.

Now Duncan's day gets worse. His secretary has to take the afternoon off because her child is suddenly sick. He is even angrier and more resentful because he is no longer in control of his world. Anger and resentment stop him from thinking clearly, which in

Exaggeration, Denial, and Pain   77

turn means that he begins to mess up the rest of the day. This gives him even more reason to be angry. The rest of the staff are now avoiding him. Behind his back they call him "Bunkum." Duncan is really stressed. He wants something to relax him, to make his mind switch off. He places another bet because if he manages to win, he will feel better. He might think that work stress has triggered his gambling, and this would be partly true. But we can see that underneath the work stress is his need to have his shaky ego propped up. If Duncan could understand how his shaky ego contributes to his work stress, then he would not need a gambling win to prop himself up. There could be a whole lot of emotional stresses affecting each of us, being a perfectionist, wanting a lot of money, needing praise, wanting to be famous, and so on. All of them are about boosting our ego, or about feeling safe.

Emotions and Desires

On the surface we can see that the exaggerated emotion comes from an unwise way of reacting to, or judging, our feelings. We add more significance to things and events because we want them so badly and so it becomes more disastrous if we miss out. We crave for the good things we do not have. We crave to be released from the bad things that might be happening to us. The problem is not the wanting, but the craving. Without this intense wanting and craving, then pleasure is enjoyed while it is there and pain is tolerated patiently.

Desire and Motivation

What makes the difference between a positive and negative desire is the quality of the motivation behind it. What could my motivation be for learning to meditate? Do I badly want this because I will be a more helpful person? That's a good motivation because everyone benefits. Do I want to be a helpful person because then everyone will think I'm so good? Not so good for me because it will inflate my pride, but maybe good for them. Do I badly want this because

I can then crawl into my corner and forget about the rest of the world? Bad for them and me. Do I want this so I can have a good rest and feel better? Maybe good. Do I want this so I can rage so much that the rest of the world no longer exists for me? No, bad for everyone. In other words, it is not *what* we do, but *why* we do it that is important. Checking our motivation in this way also means developing the wisdom to decide what is a good motivation and what is a bad motivation.

Feeling Good or Bad about Myself

Emotions become exaggerated through fear. Even when that fear is about not getting what we want, behind that is often a desperate desire to prop up a shaky self-esteem. If I have an intense desire to learn to swim, then you would probably say this is a good thing because this give me the energy to go to the pool and to practice the strokes and to develop the potential to save myself, or even save others, from drowning. If my original desire to learn to swim is forgotten and I get caught up in being excessively competitive, as Duncan might, and I begin to think that I have to win, then I will start to have problems and become stressed. How do I then feel if I do not win? How do I then feel if I do win? If my desire to win goes over the top, there is now a grasping desperation in my mind to win and not lose. I have forgotten my original reason for learning to swim. I have now put a heavy emotional load on to whether I swim well or not.

When we have these emotional investments, then we begin to judge ourselves by something outside or by what someone says about us. We are in great danger of being thrown around by events beyond our control because we have become dependent on these outside events instead of having confidence in ourselves.

Let's take a closer look at Duncan. Like everybody else, he would like to feel good about himself. He feels good about himself when he is in control and particularly when he knows the answer to anything. Secretly, he feels awful about himself and he does not like other people to know this. He feels like that because his own father constantly put him down. His Dad did that because he in turn was put down by his father, and so on. So Duncan is repeating the family history in his own way.

When Duncan can give an answer, he feels good about himself. This means that he has a major emotional investment in giving an answer—which he does all the time, whether the answer is right or wrong. When he gets it right, he feels great. He has power over other people who did not know the answer, and this is a good substitute for feeling hopeless in front of his Dad. His investment in getting the answer right is so huge that he will give any answer with an air of "I know and you don't." If he knew that people called him "Bunkum" behind his back, he would be devastated. He really annoys people a lot because he doesn't listen to them. He doesn't listen because he thinks he knows the right answer. At work he is a pain. At home he is chronically angry because he has even less control there. The less control he has, the bigger his emotional loading and the more likely he is to become angry or even violent to achieve this. So now he desperately needs his addiction.

Feeling bad about ourselves comes about because we really want to feel good. Duncan secretly feels bad about himself, but he continues to be a pain because he thinks that pretending he really does know everything *might* make him feel good. Feeling good and feeling bad go with each other. We try to feel good. It doesn't work. We feel bad. Because we feel bad, we try harder to feel good, but we're doomed. As soon as we feel good, we are haunted by feeling bad. This has come about because we do not have the balance of equanimity towards our feelings. What we really need is self-confidence, and for that we need to develop a little more wisdom.

Feeling Bad and Addiction

Even if feeling bad was not the reason for our addiction in the first place, then we start to feel bad in the end because we know we are hurting ourselves and usually hurting a lot of other people through the addiction. Feeling bad, though, may give us enough energy to make us try to get out of the addiction. Feeling bad is not necessarily a problem.

If our self-esteem is shaky, then we tend to behave irrationally, impulsively, and thoughtlessly. We are too bound up in trying to keep ourselves together to be able to think about the effect our behavior has on others. We grab at our addiction to stop this. Addictions stop us from feeling bad for the moment but they do not solve the problem

Feeling bad becomes a problem when we feel stuck. When that happens, our self-loathing and emotional pain increase. Because we feel bad, we think we are bad people. This is guilt. There is a TV program about people who are seriously fat, so fat that their lives are being threatened. Each one felt bad about not being able to stop eating. Each one of them also said how good it felt to eat this huge diet of fat and sugar. Each one felt out of control and each one was ashamed. And each one still ate an excessive amount. If they felt so bad, then why did they continue to eat? When we look underneath, we begin to see that the food problem is likely to be a distraction from an underlying problem such as feeling we are bad or unloved or jealous or angry. Guilt cannot turn around these negative perceptions of ourselves or negative emotions towards others.

Sometimes an addictive pattern came about because we have had physical or emotional pain inflicted on us through no fault of our own. Then we tend to become resentful, bitter, angry, jealous, depressed, and feeling hopeless. Negative emotions like these are like acid. They eat away at our thoughts. We might begin to imagine ways of paying back the person who hurt us. We might feel so overwhelmed that we think nothing can fix the problem. We might feel bitter towards ourselves because we must have been so bad for that person to hurt us. As the acid of these thoughts eats away at us, of course we become desperate to get away from the emotions. Addiction comes from trying to get rid of pain. We might even think of suicide. If I die from my addiction, then good, I will never again feel this terrible pain. It is not hard to see that corrosive thoughts like that are not going to help us get out of the addiction. We need tools for wiser ways of managing pain.

Some of you will have been born into families in which one or both of your parents had shaky self-esteem. If so, your parents, in turn, probably came from families that did not handle emotions in a positive way. They were affected by the fears of their own parents, just as you are affected by their fears. Abusing others is a way in which people protect themselves against their own fears and their own poor self-esteem. What does a small child think when he or she is being abused? Often it goes like, "I must be no good. They keep telling me I'm no good. What do I have to do to get their approval?"

If we are being put down or abused, then we have to find a way to deal with that. We can ignore it, or deny it, or fight back, or accept it. If we cut off our better judgment to appease the abuser, then we become cut off from ourselves. If we go our own way, then we can be abused even more. We become cut off from others and maybe even distrust everyone. Whatever solution we try, we experience the deep emotional pain of being separated within ourselves and/or being separated from others.

Addiction makes us very self-centered because when we blunt our minds from pain by our addiction, we blunt our minds also from the pain of others. We become so absorbed by the addiction that we no longer care about others. The danger of blunting our feelings towards ourselves and towards others was obvious in a staff working paper of The (United States) President's Council on Bioethics. The paper discusses the "brave pill" which was designed to stop the fears of soldiers in a war zone. The idea is that without the fear they will be much better soldiers, but there is a catch . . .

". . . these powers might make us willing to do things we might not otherwise do, or allow us to do the things we desire without shame, hesitation, or remorse: either by changing our psyche before the act by giving us the power (known in advance) to numb the sting or shame of the act after the fact. At the same time, the power to numb our memories might make us more 'accepting' creatures by altering our perception of the things we must accept. This forces us to consider the difference between forgiving and forgetting, or between forgiveness that requires soberly facing what needs to be forgiven and that which chemically alters our perception of what needs to be forgiven." [21]

In other words, if we blunt our fear for our safety, then we blunt our ability to be aware of the fears of others. We can no longer feel our own pain and we can no longer feel their pain. This warning also applies to the numbing of emotion in addiction. We run a serious risk of numbing our ability to feel the pain of others, of numbing conscience as well. The irony is that underneath the addiction is a deep human desire for connectedness and yet the addiction pushes us further and further away from genuine loving and being loved. Suicide is the ultimate numbing, but we can only face that choice if we are numb to the pain we are causing by our action.

Confidence Comes from Having a Little Wisdom: Separating Good Feedback from Bad

None of us wants to be like Duncan. It does not take much to see that his self-esteem might look good from the outside, but it is overdone, and it is on very unstable foundations. So we need to know how to develop a wiser and more firmly based self-esteem. This comes as we develop confidence in ourselves. We develop confidence in the same way that we develop self-loathing, through our contacts with others and the feedback they give us. How, then, did we get it wrong?

When we already despise ourselves, then we are overanxious about what people say. If someone tells us we're no good, then we feel awful. If someone tells us we're fantastic, then we feel great, but only for a while because we secretly feel awful anyway. We lose out either way. Our self-loathing is worse. What has gone wrong? Maybe we have chosen the wrong person to give us feedback. Someone who is jealous or angry with us is not likely to give us useful feedback. We need feedback from others and that feedback needs to have some loving wisdom in it. Perhaps we have chosen the right person to give us feedback, but we don't allow ourselves to believe it. Then the problem comes back to our own minds. We have been caught believing a fixed image of ourselves. We have been caught believing we cannot change.

If we want helpful feedback from someone else, then we use our wisdom to choose someone who can give us good feedback. If, for example, I ask for feedback from someone who is jealous of me, or someone who desperately wants my approval, am I likely to get an accurate reply? Unlikely. We need to choose people who can give us good quality feedback because they have their own lives together, and who are not biased towards either our good points or our bad points. In other words, we need to choose wise people. This also means being able to recognize wisdom. Someone in the helping professions may have no personal experience of your addiction, but because he or she has wisdom, then he or she can help you. Someone who has the same addiction but has no wisdom is not likely to be helpful. Or it could work the other way around. The professional has not developed wisdom and the recovered addict has. So how do we recognize wisdom? We see it in the personal qualities of the wise person, such qualities as humility, patience, and an ability to listen without distorting what has been said.

Even if we cannot find a wise listener, we can still give ourselves feedback. If you hate yourself, then you are giving yourself a very biased feedback. The feedback that we need from ourselves needs to be a simple and unemotional stating of facts; that is, feedback that uses the tool of equanimity: "This is how you are and what you can do," "This is how I am and what I can do." Then we bring in a little bit more wisdom: "If I can change something, then I make an effort to do so. If I can't change it, then I just accept that that is the way things are without exaggerating."

If we want to give ourselves helpful feedback, we need to check our motivations. We have to be very honest with ourselves, not in a harmful way, but with an attitude of equanimity. Am I caught up in guilt? Do I loathe myself? Do I repeat negative things to myself which just make me feel worse such as, "I am no good," "No one would want to love me," "I have to be perfect before anyone will love me," "I should know all the answers" . . . and so on?

We can also apply a little wisdom about how we view ourselves—recognizing that whatever we might feel, we are constantly changing. Whether we have low self-esteem or an inflated ego, we can change. These are nothing more than fixed ideas and an idea can always be changed. We might believe that this idea is what we really are, but that does not make it real. It is still just a belief. However bad we might feel about ourselves, this belief does not mean we are bad. It only means we might have behaved badly in the past.

Confidence comes also from the wisdom of equanimity which acknowledges the way things are, which does not rave on about how things should have been different, which asks quietly but firmly, "How did I get here? Where do I go from here and how do I get there?" As we acquire that wisdom, we are in a much better position to make sound choices, particularly towards managing pain. When we know we are making sound choices, then we have confidence in ourselves. A shaky self-esteem becomes replaced with a grounded self-confidence.

making choices and managing pain

6

My own experience [with pain] was that at almost exactly the moment when I could extend my experience of reality also to take in what I most wanted to avoid, I experienced a strange kind of peace. It wasn't optimism, and it was not an end to pain or to suffering. But it was real and true, and it sprang directly from that raw sense of inevitability and a rather chilling knowledge that sometimes events simply are not going to be pushed around by our wishes, no matter how passionate those wishes may be.
—STEPHANIE DOWRICK[22]

IN THE END, if we want to be free from the mind of addiction, we have to understand the cause of our pain and find ways to either remove it altogether or, if that is not possible, then we need to find effective strategies to live with it. Like everything else, moving away from pain needs to be done with a little wisdom.

The mind of addiction goes like this: "So I need to stop playing computer games. I'll do that, but I can't face my mind when I am not absorbed in my computer. I will take up marathon running instead." Everyone is very happy with you. You are outside getting fit and healthy. You feel great. Then surreptitiously a new thought comes in: "When I am training, I am totally absorbed. I have no awareness of any pain. Everyone is happy with me. This is great. I have to do it more . . . and more . . . and more . . ."

Keeping away from the addiction stops us getting into that particular addiction, but it does not stop the need for addiction and the need to look at the underlying pain or unhappiness behind our addiction. We either block pain or tolerate it. The pain may be real and intense and physical, but the choice to block it or bear it comes from our mind. It is our own decision. Say we have been badly injured on an isolated beach and we have no painkillers handy. What would we do then? We would have to find a way to bear that pain. We would grit our teeth, or bite on our towel, and do our best to tolerate it until the paramedics come with morphine. This means that even in severe pain we have a choice. If we cannot find a substance which will relieve the pain, we can use our mental strength to tolerate the pain.

Freedom from Pain and the Fear of Pain

Of course we want to get rid of pain and dissatisfaction. The question is, how are we going to do this? Cindy has just had another argument with her husband. She feels bad about it but she does not like feeling bad, so how is she going to get rid of this feeling? Cindy reaches for some alcohol, though someone else might reach for food or cigarettes or go to play the slot machines or look for sex. In effect, like Cindy, we are then saying that we cannot tolerate feeling bad any more. Since our addiction stops the bad feeling (at least for the moment), we then tend to fall into the addictive pattern more and more, building up the familiarity factor, which strengthens the addictive pattern. We become less able to tolerate the pain so we need our addiction even more.

Sometimes the addictive pattern involves using one pain to mask another pain. This is true for people who harm themselves, such as by pulling out hair, or cutting at flesh, or putting themselves into dangerous situations. We call them masochists. In these situations, one intense pain is able to mask another hurtful pain, such as feeling lonely, or being abused, or trapped, or feeling one is a failure, or lack of help for mental illness.

Masking pain is not always bad. For example, it is quite common for people to not experience pain just after a nasty accident. The pain comes later. Another way to mask pain is to use self-hypnosis. Painkillers such as codeine and morphine also mask pain and for that reason they can become an addiction in their own right. In the end, we need to find the cause of the pain which we are masking. If we can do that, then we can deal with our pain more effectively than through an addiction.

The Physical Pain of Withdrawal from Addiction

With many drugs and with alcohol there is an added problem—the effect of the drug and/or alcohol on the body and especially the brain. Drug dependency occurs when the addicted person needs more and more of the addictive substance in order to feel better. If you are caught in dependency on a drug, then you will also have withdrawal symptoms. Withdrawal can be painful, sometimes very painful.

The substance-dependent person now has two things to deal with. There is the pain of withdrawal *and* the pain that is being masked by the drug. If that person has no effective way of tolerating either pain, then the future is bleak and relapse becomes highly likely.

Since the pain of withdrawal is physical, then other drugs to counteract the symptoms of withdrawal can be useful. This book does not cover medical solutions, but this does not mean that medical solutions are not important. Doctors and psychiatrists have an important role. Just as important are effective mental strategies. These mental strategies can be used to modify the pain of withdrawal as well as modifying the masked pain.

The Emotional Pain of Withdrawal from Addiction

Apart from the physical withdrawal symptoms which arise when we stop a drug addiction, there are other sets of withdrawal symptoms. We are no longer masking the underlying emotional pain and so it resurfaces. This can make us feel as though everything is hopeless unless we can either remove the pain or learn to tolerate it without becoming addicted. There is also the pain that comes when people do not recognize our attempts to change, or even actively undermine them. In addiction we might begin to experience the pain of knowing the damage we have caused to ourselves and people around us.

For example, take a teenage boy who is into adrenalin hits and testosterone charges. We'll call him Flynn. How has Flynn become such a pain to everyone? It is not just the excess testosterone, but also his inability to tolerate short-term discomfort. In other words, Flynn is impulsive and probably threw temper tantrums as a kid. We say his mind is unclear, which simply means that he has not yet developed wisdom. What is the wisdom he needs? He needs to understand that life is often unfair and that this unfairness is not solved by temper tantrums or running away to get an adrenalin hit on his skateboard. If he does understand this small piece of wisdom, then he will naturally find better ways of dealing with what he dislikes in his life. The adrenalin hits are his way of avoiding the emotional pain of not getting what he wants when he wants it.

Cindy also tries to mask her pain. She was abused as a child and is now being abused by her husband. We know that for Cindy one cause of the pain comes from outside, from the person who is abusing or neglecting her. Cindy is obliged to do everything for her husband just as Cinderella was obliged to do everything for her stepmother—at least until the handsome prince turned up. Cindy also would like a handsome prince to whisk her out of reality. Everyone else knows she should leave her husband, but she won't. Her mind is unclear: distressed, unhappy. Maybe she still thinks she can change him, or she is terrified of living without the money he supplies, or maybe she likes the role of the martyr, or maybe she can't cope with the criticism she'll get when she leaves. All these attitudes are negative, unhappy, or harmful states of the mind. Her reality is also that her husband is a bully, but the only things she can change are her emotional reactions and emotional pain. If she can find a way to clear her mind from fear, then she has a possibility of choosing an appropriate solution. Alcohol gives her some relief, but she knows this is not really an answer, and she is feeling even worse about herself. Cindy would benefit a lot from the meditations on equanimity.

There are useful and harmful ways of handling the pain. If we want to do things differently, then we have to make a deliberate choice, a conscious decision. It is difficult to make that decision when the pain is severe, so what we are going to do is to train ourselves to be different. The more we practice, the better we will become. Remember, familiarity will help in making changes. In most of the meditations we imagine what things are like and how they can be different. When we use our imagination with this quiet concentration, this helps us to change what we do later.

Accept Pain or Get Relief?

It may be that the pain, like an addiction, is so overwhelming that we feel out of control. We may, in fact, be unable to control the pain, but we do have a choice as to whether we move away from the pain or move towards it. We do not need to choose one way as always right and the other way as always wrong. One strategy may be best one day and the next day we might do the opposite. Whichever we do, we need to apply the tool of equanimity.

When the pain is too much to handle, then some relief gives us space to rest and recuperate. But if we choose to numb our pain all the time, we can end up in a closed and lonely world. If we choose to face our pain, then we have the opportunity to understand its source and that helps us to be more compassionate towards others who experience pain. Taking a zealous attitude means we never give ourselves a break. We are propping up our egos rather than finding ways to heal the pain.

We need to consciously decide to mask our pain when the pain, for the moment, is too much. We need to know we can act immediately. At the same time, we need to know that blocking pain does nothing to remove the source of that pain. If we can, then it is best to find ways to remove the pain altogether. If the pain is chronic physical pain, for example, pain from scar tissue or cancer that cannot be fixed, then blocking it out gives us relief, a breathing space.

Finding Relief from Pain by Seeking Outside Help

We can get some temporary relief from pain by seeking outside help in the form of medicines, professionals working in the field, and from other people with a similar addiction.

Many people with addictions are masking depression. Certainly research shows that there is often a connection between the two.[23] It may be helpful to consult a health practitioner about depression and other psychiatric illnesses as a way of loosening the hold of your addiction. Taking antidepressants or other psychiatric drugs does not mean you are a failure. They can be an alternative way of helping you through the pain and especially if your addiction means you have withdrawal symptoms. With the help of such drugs you are then in a better position to use other strategies suggested here or by a counselor or self-help group.

Getting help from outside means getting help to relieve the immediate pain. We also need help to get to the source of the pain, whether the pain has a physical cause, because something is wrong with our bodies, or a mental cause. Getting help from outside is one way of developing our wisdom minds. But at the same time, from our side we need to *choose* to be open to being helped and we need to *choose* to take the medicine, to change the way we do things. It also helps to apply some wisdom in choosing who to ask for help.

Finding Relief from Pain by Using the Mind: Blocking Pain

We can get some distance from pain through blocking it or dissociating from it. We do this by concentrating intensely so that the awareness of pain cannot get through to our consciousness. Hypnosis is a good example of dissociation. If we allow ourselves to go into a hypnotic trance, then during the trance we are aware only of what is happening in our mind and totally unaware of things happening around us. It is even possible to have operations done under hypnosis without the use of any anesthetic.

There are many ways of keeping our mind so occupied that we are unaware of the pain. This happens because our mind is limited in what it can do, so if it is totally occupied with one thing, it can be totally unaware of anything else. Kids in front of the TV can be like that. They just do not hear their parents when they are called to dinner. Watching a good video, reading a good book, playing a musical instrument, weeding the garden, knitting . . . anything that does not require much in the way of a response from us can be used in this way. It is mindfulness put to good use. We decide that we are going to be mindful only of what we are doing and nothing else, including any pain.

A student in a workshop told me about her experience with blocking pain. She had to have a deep splinter removed from her foot and the wound stitched. The doctor advised anesthetics, but she refused because she had previously reacted badly to them. To block the pain she concentrated very strongly on a crack in the wall. Everything went well. She could feel that there was something happening to her foot, but she did not allow herself to identify with her foot. Then the nurse touched her and said, "Are you all right, dear?" At that moment the student lost her concentration and the pain came flooding back! She then had to concentrate even harder on the crack in the wall to stop herself from feeling the pain.

Training in self-hypnosis or mindfulness can be helpful in moving away from pain. Strong mindfulness, say, of a pleasant breeze, means less space in the mind to be aware of pain. In doing this next meditation it is important to remember that moving away from pain should never be your main strategy for dealing with pain. We actually need pain to tell us what is wrong. We move away from pain to give us a break when the pain has become too much.

We can also dissociate from the pain by seeing it as "not me." Pain really gets to us when we feel that we are nothing but pain and can do nothing about it. We are overwhelmed by it. Not identifying with pain can happen when people are in a bad accident. They do not feel the pain until later, even though they might be seriously hurt. Their burns, or shattered limbs, or pools of blood are noticed, but as something other than themselves. They do not yet identify with the injury. That comes later.

So we can teach ourselves to not identify with the pain. This also has to be done with some wisdom. If we simply deny the pain, then we do not achieve anything. What we do is to recognize the pain, but to see that the pain is not central to being "me." To do that we have to stop and think what it means to be "me," what I mean by "I." So we investigate. Am I just my body? No, because I also think. Am I just my mind? No, because I also have a body. Am I some combination of my body and mind? Well, this seems to get us a little closer. But how can I be a combination of my body and mind if I am neither my body nor my mind? What am I? Who am I? These are philosophical questions.

Buddhism says that there is no thing called "me" that can be identified. We cannot identify any one element of a city, say Melbourne, as being Melbourne, yet we know that Melbourne exists. Melbourne does not exist as a thing, but as an idea which we all agree should be called "Melbourne."

When we are trapped in a lot of pain, it is difficult to see that the pain is "not-me." We can feel that we are nothing but pain. But when we stop to think about it, then we know that we are more than the pain. If we learn to stop identifying with the pain, then we can begin to observe the pain for what it actually is and make use of equanimity. I can look at my injured arm or recall feeling abandoned as a child without feeling that I am disintegrating as a person.

Anything which keeps your mind strongly occupied can help you move away from pain. Mindfulness is the word we use when we focus our attention on just one thing. Concentration means that the mindfulness is intensely focused. You can choose what that thing might be. Here are some suggestions you can use as your focus for mindfulness:

You can imagine yourself somewhere pleasant. If you do this vividly, then your mind loses awareness of the pain.

You can meditate strongly on the suffering of people who experience even more pain than you do.

You can keep your mind on your breathing and absolutely nothing else.

You can meditate strongly on what your life will be like without your addiction.

You can maintain your awareness of being in the pure compassionate wisdom energy and allow nothing else to enter your mind.

You can focus on a crack in the wall.

You can imagine yourself as you lie in your bed, surrounded by pure compassionate wisdom.

Meditation 8: I Am Not My Pain

When pain becomes overwhelming, we feel as if we are nothing but pain: it will always be there. If we reflect, then we find that this is not true. Sometimes it feels bad and at other times it is not so bad. If we have done the breathing and relaxing exercises from Chapter 2, then we have, for that time, distracted our mind from the pain and so felt some relief. Now we meditate specifically to dissociate ourselves from pain. This is an analytical meditation. We think about the logic, and then stay with the implications of what we have thought out.

If I am not my pain, then I can separate my pain from my emotions. I do not need to be irritable or depressed just because I am in pain.

Melbourne is constantly changing. I am constantly changing. Just as there is no one building that can be called "Melbourne," there is no one part of "me" that can be called "me." I can correctly label my body and mind as "me" and yet I cannot identify any one part as "me." If no one part of me is "me," then my pain is not "me."

Motivation

Once again we think about our personal reason for doing the meditation. This time we also try to see how our own agenda can also benefit other people. We then put this into our own words and keep it firmly in our mind. Our motivation might be: "I do not like being in pain and I need some relief from this. Even a small moment of relief will give me some space to see my life in perspective and this will be helpful for myself and the people around me."

Tuning in to pure compassionate wisdom

This is an important part of your meditation. It corresponds to the reliance on a Higher Power used in the twelve steps of Alcoholics Anonymous. As we rest in this pure compassionate wisdom, we allow ourselves to be guided by that energy,

The meditation

First think about various parts of your body. If your arm were cut off, would you still be you? What about your leg, or your ear? What if your heart were to be cut out? Then you would die. On the other hand, you can manage without a large part of your stomach.

Think: "My body is important to me. I could not exist without some of its essential elements. But is my body me?" Stay with this thought for a while.

Now contemplate your mind. If you lose your memory, are you still you? If you can no longer find your way home, are you still you? What about when you are asleep? Or knocked unconscious? Or drunk? What if you were afflicted with Alzheimer's disease? Would you still be you?

Think: "My mind seems more essential to being 'me' than my body does. Still, I can do without some parts of my mind and still be 'me.' What is this 'me'?" Pause to contemplate this idea.

That part of ourselves that we call "me" is not the whole of my body, nor is it the whole of my mind. What is it then? Is it something other than my body and mind?

If no one part of me is "me," then my pain is not "me." I do not have to stick to one fixed concept of "me." I am not my pain.

Stay with any insight that may come as a result of doing this meditation

Closing the meditation

As before, think about any benefits you have received from doing this meditation. These benefits come from the source of pure compassionate wisdom, which is the same as your own mind in its completely purified state.

Dedication

Make the decision to use any nuggets of wisdom to help you on your path to breaking the addiction trap—not just so that you will feel better, but so you can be in a position to benefit other people who suffer, especially the ones who suffer even more than you.

Moving Towards Pain

When we have pain, the temptation is to want to ward it off, or push it away. This builds up resistance and tightness in body and mind and often makes the pain worse. This is true for both physical and mental pain. Moving towards the pain means making the decision to be completely open to it instead of masking it. This may seem crazy when you have spent so much time, energy, and probably money trying to get away from it. But we can be quite surprised by the results. Moving towards pain means allowing ourselves to be totally aware of what the pain is really like. We can train our minds to do this at times when the pain is not so bad. Then as we continue to practice, we become more tolerant of pain during the bad times.

If we are frightened, or depressed, or feeling that we are worth nothing, then physical pain can seem to be much worse than it actually is. We are exaggerating the pain. What we are thinking, our expectations, affects the degree to which we feel pain. Have you ever picked up a hot object thinking it was cold? It takes longer for the burning sensation to hit your mind because you are thinking, "This is not hot." Another example is food. You think you are eating a potato and so you taste potato. Then you begin to think that the potato has a funny taste. It was not a potato, but a parsnip.

Our awareness of sensations is strongly affected by our expectations. Say, for example, that you have to have an injection, but you are afraid of pain. You screw up your courage and wait for the pain to hit. As soon as you feel a slight touch you jump, thinking about the pain. It was the nurse swabbing your arm. But by now your arm is tense, your mind is tense, and when the needle goes in you feel a lot of pain. Imagine, instead, that you go to have the injection feeling very relaxed. When the swab touches your arm you just feel the cold sensation. When the needle goes in you feel it going into your arm and yes, there is some pain, but it is minor and temporary. By the time the needle comes out you only feel a slight sting. Of course some injections are much more painful than others. The point I am making here is that even a minor injection will feel painful if we are expecting it to be painful and we are exaggerating around it. The opposite also applies. Even a major injection will be less painful if we are not making the pain worse by imagining a disaster.

Moving towards pain means having the courage to be completely open to it and we develop this courage as we develop equanimity

Meditation 9: Accepting Pain

First we meditate on the physical aspect of any pain we might have. It can be helpful to use this meditation to help with withdrawal symptoms. In this meditation we go into the pain, explore it, and become more aware of what it really feels like. At first this may seem frightening, but it usually reduces any fear because we know exactly what we are facing rather than running away from it.[24]

You might find it helpful to lie down when you do this meditation so that your body can be as relaxed as possible. But be careful that you do not fall asleep instead of meditating! Whether you are sitting or lying, try to have your body symmetrical around your spine.

Close your eyes and relax. The breathing exercises can help you do this, or you may have learned other relaxation meditations. Relax in whatever way works for you.

Motivation

As you relax, think also about your motivation for doing this meditation. Here is another suggestion for your motivation. Think: "I am doing this meditation so that I can have some relief from my pain and my body can be healthy. There is no point in having a healthy body if I use it to harm others and harm myself. So I am doing this meditation so that I can be healthy and to bring wisdom and kindness to others and to myself. If I am to bring wisdom and kindness, then I must access their source."

Tuning in to pure compassionate wisdom
Take some time to feel that you are in the presence of wisdom and kindness. It is helpful to see the source of such a pure mind in a human form. You can imagine that rays of light come from that source. Think that with the help of this energy I can summon my courage and look directly at my pain.

Imagining the pain
You may have various pains in your body. Choose just one of these and later repeat the meditation for other pain you might have.

Where is my pain?
Move your attention through the body, seeking out that area that gives you pain. Be as specific as possible. Is it close to the skin? Deep inside your body? In your head, or your chest, or your limbs, or your trunk? Exactly where is this sensation?

Rest in that awareness for a time

How big is my pain?
Does this pain affect a large part of your body or a small part? Try to narrow it down as much as you can. Be aware of its size. How long? How wide? How deep?

Rest in that awareness for a time

If I could see my pain, what would it look like?
Be aware of its shape. Is it like a ball? A rod? A lump? A spear?

Be aware of its density. Is it solid or frothy? Heavy or light? Is it the same all the way through?

What surface texture does it have? Is it soft, fuzzy, smooth, rough? What does it feel like?

What is its temperature? Hot or cold, or the same as the rest of your body?

Does it have a color? What color do you imagine it could be?

Healing the pain with wisdom and kindness

Now focus on your breath. We will use our breath as healing energy. We can imagine it bringing oxygen molecules to where they are needed. We can also imagine our breath carrying the healing rays of wisdom and kindness into our bodies.

For the first three rounds of breathing:

Imagine that your breath washes the affected part of your body and eases the pain. Then let the breath gently ebb away with each exhalation. As you breathe gently out, imagine the pain is also leaving your body.

For the next three rounds of breathing:

Imagine that the breath is drawn inside the pain, washing the inside, and the pain ebbing away with each exhalation.

For the final three rounds of breathing:

We imagine the breath once again washing both outside and inside the affected area and pain. We continue breathing in this way for a while, noting any changes, or lack of change, with equanimity.

Take a moment to reflect on what has happened, even if nothing has happened. No change does not mean that we are no good at meditating. No change in one meditation does not mean no change the next time we do it. If this meditation has given us a lot of insight, then we can be happy. If any of us find no insight in the next meditation, then there is no cause to worry. We simply note what has happened with equanimity.

Closing the meditation

Take some time to think about the effects this meditation has had for you. Be happy that you have had the time and space to do the meditation. Be aware again that wisdom and kindness surround you.

Dedication

Here is another example of a dedication. You can write your own if you prefer.

Think: "I have done this meditation so that I can have a clearer awareness of my pain. This clarity is the basis for being able to understand my pain. It is an effect which has had a cause. It changes, and since it changes, it will not be this way forever.

"As I apply equanimity to my pain and my meditation, I become aware of my own suffering. If I suffer in this way, I can be sure that other people suffer in the same way. Some of these people have much worse experiences than I do. By being aware of my own pain, I am more keenly aware of their pain.

"To all people who suffer as I do, I send out the positive energy I have developed in my mind by doing this meditation. May they find relief from their pain and happiness in their lives."

Making Choices and Building Self-Confidence

Knowing that we have a choice makes a big difference in how we feel about ourselves. In one sense this book is all about making choices. When we know that we can make choices and when we actually carry them through, then we start to build a sound confidence in ourselves. A sound confidence is realistic. It comes from knowing clearly what we can and cannot do. For example, for some people their pain is chronic. Perhaps it comes from an accident or illness, or from emotional trauma which cannot be removed. In this case, it is sound reasoning to say, "I cannot remove this pain because . . ." For other people, the pain may be exaggerated by fear or by a belief that it cannot be changed. Maybe they are too used to being a victim. Maybe they think they cannot build up enough emotional strength and courage. Maybe they think they will always be weaker than others. In these cases, they may use the same words: "I cannot remove this pain because . . ." But the reasoning is faulty. Faulty reasoning does not build a sound self-confidence.

So if we want to be able to make choices, we need to look carefully and clearly at the reasons why we have not taken that choice in the past. We need to investigate our beliefs and see whether they hold true or not. That also means that we need to check out what our beliefs really are. When we check out our beliefs and go deeper and deeper into them, we find ourselves questioning things like the meaning of life. When we start to find the sources of compassionate wisdom, we begin to reflect on our humanistic and spiritual and religious beliefs.

Whichever way we approach addiction, we have both short-term and long-term things that we need to work on. We do not need to do only one or only the other. We can choose. We can choose whether to avoid the pain for a time or to face the pain for a time, and investigate how our minds react to it. Addiction makes us feel as though we have lost the power to choose, but we can reclaim this power.

Meditation 10: Choosing to Change, Being Kind to Ourselves

Any negative emotional state is painful. Anger, greed, jealousy, fear, arrogance, envy, depression, and so on come from misery, but they also bring more misery. Emotions might come from our mind, but we hold them in our bodies. We might be tense in the head, or neck, or stomach, or arm—in fact we can be tense almost anywhere in our bodies. One of the worst of emotional pains is self-loathing.

We meditate on this emotional pain in the same way that we do with the physical pain. This time we check to see where we hold the emotional tension and use that part of our body for the meditation.

It is very important that this meditation is done with equanimity. If we focus deliberately on emotional pain, we could easily aggravate it instead of healing it. The pain can become aggravated when we lack wisdom. Without wisdom we might exaggerate the emotional pain because thinking about it might make us angry or fearful or depressed.

Sometimes I say to people doing this meditation to be like a loving mother nursing a sick child. Moms mop up the vomit, change the sheets, nurse the crying child. Be the kind Mom to yourself even if you have never been—or had—a Mom like that.

Although we are liable to blame someone else for being too hard on us, mostly we are too hard on ourselves. This meditation helps to change that.

Motivation

First we remember to check out our motivation for doing the meditation. Whatever we individually need, we also make sure to include the needs of others so they will also benefit from us doing the meditation. We can use one of the motivations from a previous meditation or we can make up our own.

Tuning in to pure compassionate wisdom

Each time we do this, we reinforce the thought that this compassionate wisdom is what we need so that we can ourselves act wisely and compassionately.

The meditation

We imagine that we are about to begin our addictive pattern: that moment when we reach out our hand, or open a cupboard, or walk into a room, or head out to the shops. Imagine how strong the urge for the addiction is at that moment for each of us. Now we each imagine our own scene . See yourself there as vividly as you can. Now think that someone comes in and smacks your hand away, or slams the cupboard door, or shoves you out of the room . . . whatever is necessary to stop you from getting whatever you want so much. That person is so angry with you. How do you react to that person? Think how angry you would be, how bitter and resentful. Or maybe you would feel guilty or hopeless. Imagine your own reaction as strongly as you can.

Now imagine the same thing, but this time the person who stops

you is yourself. One part of you is desperate for the addiction. The
other part of you says you should not have it. The part that is desperate for the addiction is bitter and angry towards the part that says
you should not have it. We both want to change and resent change.
This is a big reason why we cannot give up the addiction. There is
so much anger from the part of us that knows we should stop. And
there is so much anger from the part of us that resents having to
stop. We are stuck! Think about this for a while.

Now we change the meditation. This time, think about a person
who has been very kind to you and only has your interests at heart.
It may be someone you know, or knew. It may be someone in your
imagination. This person is kind and fair, but firm. Now once again
imagine that you are about to indulge and the urge for your addiction is very strong. This person who really has your best interests
at heart sees you, and stops you, firmly but kindly. How does this
change your reactions? What do you feel now towards someone
who really loves you? Do you still feel angry? Do you feel sad? Does
your heart break because you are now being loved?

This time imagine the same scene except that the person who
has your interests at heart is the wise part of yourself. Your wise
self is kind and fair, but firm. Your wise self knows your pain and
accepts it. The wise self knows that you are looking for relief and
accepts that. The wise self knows that above all you need to be loved
for what you are. How do you feel towards this wise self which is
you?

Stay with your thoughts about this for a while. Think how this
wise self is your own wisdom and your own loving-kindness.

Closing the meditation

Now we tune once again in to wisdom and kindness, recognizing
that our own wisdom and loving-kindness have the same qualities.
Whatever wisdom we may have developed during the meditation,
we remember it now and decide to keep it in our mind. Whatever
each of us feels we might need to do as a result of this meditation,
we each think about how we might do just that.

Dedication

Now rest quietly and happily because you have had the opportunity to meditate in this way. Remember why you are doing the meditation and dedicate the positive effects to achieving that goal.

cleaning out rubbish: forgiveness

7

The question is not "to forgive" or "not to forgive." This question will not help us find a breakthrough in our habit of dualistic thinking: oneself vs. the others, good vs. evil, right vs. wrong. A more helpful question would be, "How can I better understand myself and the other person?"
—ANH-HUONG[*]

CHANGING OUR LIFE is like moving into a new house. We clean out the rubbish from the old house so we can make a new start. When we want to change our lives it is much the same: we need to clean out the rubbish from our minds, to get rid of the useless stuff. Hanging on to the useless stuff is bad for our physical as well as our mental health. Addiction means facing up to any damage which we might have caused to ourselves and others from our past behavior and then cleaning up our act, otherwise we are living in a fantasy world.

Cleaning out the rubbish means that we pay attention to our conscience, that part of our humanity that knows when we are hurting others. Our conscience is the little angel that sits on one shoulder and is in constant dispute with the devil on the other shoulder. The devil is our self-serving ego that does not care about other people. The angel is concerned about those values which are important for the lasting happiness of ourselves and others. The self-serving ego, the devil, is not concerned with long-term benefits, only with immediate short-term benefits. The devil says, "Get what you can and forget about the downside." He is not concerned with values. The sorts of values that the angel wants for us are those which show us how to behave so that everyone benefits, such as the values listed in the Ten Commandments of Christianity or the eightfold noble path of Buddhism.

Addiction means that the devil has the stronger voice and ends up causing a lot of damage. One important part of breaking the addiction trap is to be honest with ourselves and freely admit that we have created harm. This does not mean that we need to fall into endless recrimination. Instead we apply equanimity towards our feelings as we did in Chapter 3.

Once we admit to our failings, we are then able to face them directly and make a decision to be different. To help us do that we learn to forgive ourselves, and to be forgiven by others. We can forgive ourselves when we have courage, wisdom, a dose of humility, and a kindly acceptance of what we are at this moment, good and bad. We need these values even more when we want to be forgiven by people we have hurt. They may be too angry to be kind to us.

Being forgiven does not mean that people we have harmed are not hurt. Rather, it says that the slate is now clean, that the past has gone and it is the future which is more important. We can start again. Not everyone will be able to forgive us, but we will be forgiven by people who have hope in our courage and wisdom.

For the forgiveness to have meaning, we need to find ways of doing things differently so that we do not cause further harm in the future. There are two ways of doing this. Firstly, it means finding ways to undo the harm we have caused where it is possible. Secondly, it means finding an opposite and positive action to replace the harmful one, such as replacing greed with generosity. As we do that, we are creating new habits and patterns that have a beneficial effect to replace the addictive patterns which had a harmful effect. We are giving more power to the angel and less to the devil.

Forgiving and Being Forgiven: The Story of Carri

Forgiveness is not an easy option, whether we try to forgive ourselves or to forgive people who may have harmed us. Let's look at another story, this time about Carri. There are three versions of this story because we do not know what Carri's future will be.

For a long time Carri had lied to her parents, had stolen from them, had sworn at them, and told them they were worse than useless. They knew she was into drugs, but whatever they did, nothing seemed to help. Carri is now struggling to be drug-free and is feeling bad about what she has said and done in the past. She is making a courageous effort to face up to the effects of her addiction and to the difficulties of withdrawal. She wants herself to be different and she wants her parents to appreciate and love her. She wants them to forgive her.

Version 1

Carri is at her parents' home finishing the evening meal. She says, "Things will be different now. I'm giving up drugs."

Her parents say, "You've said that before."

"But I mean it this time."

"You expect us to believe you? Look what you've done in the past. Look how we tried to help you and you threw it back at us. You came up to us all sweetness and smiles and said exactly what you're saying now. Go away. We don't want to go through all that again."

Carri is hurt. "So you've just proved how right I was. Whatever I do is never good enough for you."

Now Carri loses it entirely. She swears at her parents and storms off in a huff. She is hurting and needs something to stop her pain. Where will she get this? From her addiction? Probably. Remember she is still struggling to be drug-free and is not always successful.

It could have been different. We'll try a different version. It starts the same way but goes off in a different direction, largely because Carri has been doing some more work on breaking her addictive patterns and has been practicing equanimity.

Version 2

Carri goes to her parents. "Things will be different now."

"You've said that before."

"But I mean it this time."

"You expect us to believe you? Look what you've done in the past. Look how we tried to help you and you threw it all back at us. You came up to us all sweetness and smiles and said exactly what you're saying now. Go away. We don't want to go through all that again."

This time Carri brings in the equanimity tool. She can feel the pattern of anger arising, but she makes a deliberate decision to remain calm. She has already thought about what to do if her parents do not believe her. She says, "You're right. I have been a big mess to live with. I'm sorry."

There is silence. She has said, "Sorry." Her parents don't know what to say. They just look at her. Can they really trust her? They're not too sure. They've been hurt before. What if this is just another of Carri's tricks? She watches their faces, herself hovering between a temper tantrum and repeating her apology. After all, she is not yet an expert in equanimity. How can she make them believe her? How can she get them to see she is really trying this time? She fidgets with her sleeve. She doesn't know what to say either.

Still there is silence. Her parents have never seen her quite like this. She has never been quite like this before. She mumbles again, "I'm sorry."

The effect of Carri's past behavior is easy to see. Her parents do not trust her because when they did in the past, their trust was abused. This has happened so often that her parents are still not going to trust her. The probability is that she is fooling them again. But on the other hand, she is being different. She has said, "Sorry." Her behavior is different. Are her parents able to handle that? Maybe yes, maybe no. Carri has got at least a little further ahead, but her parents have still not responded the way she would like them to. They are caught in their own past habits and they have plenty of reason to be wary.

Carri is not perfect and she sometimes gets things right and sometimes doesn't; from her point of view she is doing the right thing this time. "Why," she thinks, "don't they trust me? Can't they see what I am trying to do?" No, they cannot. They still think she is fooling them.

Do they live happily ever after? Not in this story, at least not yet. There is a lot of rubbish for Carri to get rid of in her mind and the same for her parents.

We can see from this story that there needs to be love and forgiveness on both sides, and above all, patience. Carri is finding it hard to convince her parents that she really does want to change. The effect of her past behavior is that her parents learned (rightly) to mistrust her. What she is receiving now had been put in place in the days when she did deceive her parents. This is simple cause and effect. This is karma.

Carri cannot force her parents to be different even though she might have made a definite decision from her side to change. What can she do? She cannot undo her own past. Carri has to take on the responsibility for cleaning up the mess from her side. So what does this mean?

Carri needs to accept her parents for what they are now. Not for what they might be or could have been. In other words she needs to practice equanimity towards her parents.

The story continues. Carri's parents have their own rubbish to deal with, going way back to before Carri was born. They were not very skilled parents. They can't handle the change in their daughter. They feel guilty, and because they feel guilty they become angry. They throw their own temper tantrum. They push her out of the house again. But Carri is now seeing things differently. She can see that they have their own stuff to deal with and her stuff is too much for them. She sighs. She would like her parents to be different, but they are not. She knows they cannot control their own minds. Because she is now practicing equanimity, she decides to accept the situation and her parents as they are instead of getting angry because they do not respond the way she would like them to.

Carri goes to her own home and cries. She is grieving for what could be. Her parents were themselves victims of abuse from the time they were kids. She becomes sad. She can now see that they are suffering as much as she has suffered. This grief and sadness that come with acceptance are also the emotions of forgiveness. Forgiveness does not deny the past, but recognizes the other person as a victim. It is the beginning of compassion. Maybe she will never see them again, but her own mind is at peace.

Version 3

Let's try a third version. In this version, Carri's parents have not been so traumatized by their own past. Carri, as before, wants forgiveness from her parents. She sees that they may be open to change if she is different herself. She goes back. She is not craving forgiveness, but she would still like to be forgiven. Each time she goes back she is simply her new self. Not a perfect new self, but one that is different from the old one because it is trying to develop habits with positive and realistic intentions.

Her parents begin to see that indeed she is different. They accept her for who she is and admire her efforts to change. Now forgiveness comes from their side, and with it grief for what might have been and sadness for her suffering. They have always had that grief and sadness, but now Carri is able to see that. In turn, she feels grief and sadness about what she has done to herself and for the hurt she has caused to her parents. She in turn recognizes and forgives her parents for the harsh way they were forced to treat her. They were not to blame. She had set them up. Forgiveness towards her parents is mixed with shame towards herself.

This version is, of course, the ideal version and is possible only if both Carri and her parents are capable of emotional maturity. Whichever scene is true for Carri, she now is feeling deep sadness for what she has done from her side. She knows how and when she has caused harm to other people. She can see that her mind was so trapped in her own needs that she did not care what effect she had on anyone else. Now Carri needs to forgive herself or she might be swamped by self-pity and guilt.

Forgiving Ourselves

The emotions that go with forgiveness towards oneself are grief and sadness, rather than guilt and shame. We become aware that we also have been victims: not so much victims of outside events, even though these might contribute to our pain, but victims of our clenching possessiveness which wants whatever it desires, preferably immediately. It is the grip of this clenching possessiveness which blinds us to our effect on others and gives rise to anger when it is thwarted. If we can forgive ourselves, then that clenching loosens. We become less caught by our inner demands and less angry when thwarted. To put it simply, we become nicer people to live with. We are getting rid of some of the rubbish in our minds.

Sometimes this forgiveness of oneself is more effective when shared with another person, preferably someone with some wisdom. If there is no one you can trust like that, then perhaps you can offer your shame and guilt to the source of pure compassionate wisdom, whatever that might mean to you: God or Buddha or Allah or Krishna or universal love. Tuning in to pure compassionate wisdom is another way of getting rid of rubbish. Our minds become filled with the same pure compassionate wisdom instead of being filled with hate and resentment and ignorant blindness to the suffering of others.

Forgiveness towards our own behavior is not of much value unless we also promise ourselves to do things differently as much as possible. Instead of getting angry, we can try to quietly accept that the person who annoys us so much is suffering from his/her own side. Of course, if we can prevent that person from suffering, then we do what we can instead of getting angry. Taking responsibility for our own thoughts and actions also helps to clean out the rubbish because we then try to behave in an ethical way, that is, in a way that causes no harm to others.

If it is possible, then we can also undo some of the damage we have done. If we have stolen, then perhaps we can repay the person we stole from, at least in part. If we have been nasty, then we can apologize and take on the responsibility of trying not to behave in that way in the future. If we have been lying, then perhaps we can tell the truth. Even if we cannot undo old lies, at least we can take on the responsibility of being truthful in the future. If our pride has caused harm, then we can learn humility. If our ignorance has led us into trouble, then we can develop wisdom. More rubbish has been cleaned out. Taking responsibility now means being responsible for fixing up the damage we have caused wherever it is possible.

One of the most powerful ways of undoing the effects of our shameful behavior is to help others in a similar boat. Alcoholics Anonymous is a good example of how effective it is to turn our knowledge of our past into a way to help other people suffering in a similar way.

These actions—feeling a deep sense of regret, deciding to keep in touch with pure compassionate wisdom, trying to repair any damage we have done, and trying to do the opposite of whatever has been behind our thoughtless and damaging behavior—help to clean out the unwanted rubbish in our minds and strengthen the voice of the angel.

We are not only undoing harmful habits from the past, but we are also turning our minds towards the needs of others. We are becoming compassionate. We become connected in a way that had seemed impossible. As we become connected, we then find happiness creeping in where there had been misery before.

Once the rubbish has been cleaned up then there is space for the things we appreciate; that is, provided we do not collect more rubbish. Rather than putting more rubbish in, it is better to fill our minds with the little bits of wisdom. This means taking time to sit down and think about some of these things and how they affect our lives.

Meditation 11: Cleaning Rubbish from the Mind and Making Sure It Does Not Come Back

This meditation is similar to the spa bath meditation in Chapter 1. Instead of feeling the oxygen invigorating us, we visualize pure compassionate wisdom being carried on the in-breath. To do that, we make the conscious decision to tune in to pure compassionate wisdom. Then we take that energy into our bodies and minds.

Motivation
First we make sure that our motivation is a positive one. For example, "I am doing this meditation so I can clear out the rubbish from my mind. With a clear mind and heart I can be a better person. If I am a better person, then I can really help other people to do the same. I want to continue to do this until my mind is perfectly clear and wise and compassionate. Then I can be really skillful in helping others."

Tuning in to compassionate wisdom
Now we bring into our mind the source of all pure compassionate wisdom. If we can, we see this source in a human form which we will call the Divine Being so that the meditation fits different religious traditions. The Divine Being radiates an endless source of white light from the Holy Body. This white light is pure compassionate wisdom.

Feel that the Divine Being is so happy to see you and so happy that you want to receive the blessing of compassionate wisdom. Stay with this feeling of being in the presence of the Divine Being and being blessed by this.

Recognizing our faults honestly
Now in front of the goodness of the Divine Being we naturally become so ashamed of the various harms that we have caused to others and to us. We now understand how these harms have separated us from our own compassionate wisdom. We admit to them freely and honestly and with a sense of deep shame.

Receiving healing energy and forgiveness
The Divine Being, through the power of compassion, does not condemn us but instead is so happy that we can see what we need to change. Now through our honesty we have opened up and the

white healing light can come into our body and mind, heart and soul. This is the healing light of forgiveness which recognizes that however much our mind has been filled with hatred or confusion or depression or jealousy or any other negative thoughts, we have the potential to change, to develop the same pure compassionate wisdom which is flooding through our body and mind.

We stay with this healing forgiveness for a while.

Repairing the harm

Now that we have been filled with pure compassionate wisdom, we begin to realize that to keep this purity we must try to avoid making the same mistakes. This means putting positive habits in place of the negative ones. Where it is possible, we each make a commitment to repair any harm we have created. This might mean paying back what has been stolen, being kind where we had been angry, cleaning the house instead of leaving it dirty, and so on.

In the presence of this Divine Being, we now make a promise that we know we can keep, even if only for a few hours, or a few days. That is, the promise is based on the reality of who each of us is now and where we live and what we are realistically able to do. Each time we do this meditation, we can make the same promise or a new one. Whatever the promise, it is between each of us and the Holy Being.

Feel that the Divine Being is so happy with our efforts. The white light continues to pour through each of us, removing all the negative parts of our body and mind. We become more and more radiant as we absorb this light.

Replacing the harmful habits

Now that we are full of pure compassionate wisdom, there is no need to repeat the harmful behavior that we have confessed. We make another commitment, this time to do our best to stop repeating this behavior—and a third commitment to try to replace the harm with its opposite. Where we have been angry, we might decide to build the habit of patience. Where we have been selfish, we might try to be generous. Where we have lied, we might decide to be truthful.

Again, we need to be realistic in making these promises. There is no point in promising to suddenly become perfect because you know this is not possible. Instead, we find some small, positive habit which we can create now and according to who we are, who we live with, and where we live. Remembering all this, then make your promise in the presence of the Divine Being.

Once again, feel that the Divine Being is so happy with us making these efforts and that we are given all the tools and wisdom we need in order to bring our promises to fruition.

Closing the meditation

Think: "What a precious opportunity I have had, and not only that, I have had this opportunity because I chose to do this meditation."

Dedication

Then remember the motivation you chose for this meditation and think, "Even though I have not yet achieved all that I would like to, may I develop compassionate wisdom quickly and may I do all I can to bring this about."

Panning for Gold

It is not hard to see that as we work to get rid of the nasty parts of ourselves, people begin to like us more. Of course this does not mean that we go to the opposite extreme and let people walk all over us. It does mean that we become less likely to fall into bitterness or revenge, or depression or anything else that might contribute to our self-loathing. This also means that we even come to like ourselves better.

The barrier that we had set up within our minds to keep the self-loathing away from our awareness becomes unnecessary. This has an important outcome. We begin to see that what we loathed about ourselves might also have a useful purpose. For example, some of us might be compliant people, and anger would probably be part of our self-loathing. For those of us like that, any time we got angry we would hate ourselves. But now we are using equanimity. Instead of exaggerating our badness, we simply note that we are angry. Without the self-loathing, anger loses its power to destroy us. In fact, we might begin to realize that the energy which had ended up as anger is very useful when we need to express our own point of view in a group. If others have exaggerated the idea of being, say, an athlete, then they would probably think of physical weakness as part of their self-loathing. Without the exaggerations of our insecure ego, we begin to see that what seems to be weakness was actually a way of being gentle towards ourselves and others. It can be very useful to work out for each of us what our exaggerated strengths and exaggerated weaknesses might be.

When we apply equanimity towards ourselves, then we find that we reconnect with those parts of our self which we had pushed aside. As we reconnect with the hidden and despised part of ourselves, we begin to reconnect with other people. When we reconnect in this way, we begin to hope, we begin to see that there is some gold amongst the rubbish in our minds. Our lives begin to have meaning.

There is no point in finding a way out of our addictions if that means our lives are going to be boring and meaningless. It makes sense then to think about what we want in place of the addiction. Another addiction would just be pointless. We want happiness. This means that we are faced with two questions. Firstly, what is happiness? Secondly, how do we get to be happy? As part of that search for new ways of living we can check out what other people have done—not just any other person, but the people we admire because they seem to have deep satisfaction in their lives. What are their qualities?

Happiness is connected to wisdom. It can even be found amongst appalling conditions. Brian Keenan was kept as a hostage for five years by Islamic militants. During this time he became aware of the inner nature of courage and this transformed his life. He writes,

"This journey ends like all journeys. That the human mind can travel in those dark regions and return exhausted but intact is more a miracle than that word can ever convey."[26]

We find happiness when our lives are full of meaning. Our lives are full of meaning when we are connected within ourselves and with other people, with our environment, and with the energies of pure compassionate wisdom. Instead of trying to work out how to do this from our own limited wisdom, we can investigate what wise people do, how they got to be wise, and what brings meaning into their lives.

One of the images used by the Buddha to describe the incredible potential of our mind is that it is like a gold nugget buried in dirt. We do not even recognize the gold because of the dirt. Finding wisdom is like washing off the dirt and seeing the glimpse of gold. In other words, whatever the pain or problem that we might have faced or are currently facing, we can find some value as we wash it away. What seemed to be a problem can become a source of happiness.

Even when we are in a situation that might be unfair, we can still look for the gold. Take Carri, whom we met earlier in this chapter. She is trying to prove to her parents that she is really different. They can't yet see that. What is her gold nugget in all that? Well, she can learn to be patient towards others, to see that they cannot change instantly just because she has changed. She can become patient towards herself, so that when she loses it and throws a temper tantrum about her parents, she can be forgiving towards herself rather than losing herself in guilt. Patience is another speck of gold showing through the dirt.

Maybe at first we do not recognize the gold. It looks like common gravel, another bit of dirt to throw away. And let's say a geologist comes along and sees what we have thrown out and says, "Look what you've done. You've thrown away the gold." We would be so grateful to that geologist and his or her wisdom about minerals. We need the wisdom of people who have faced up to and solved the same problems that we are finding difficult. Bringing wisdom into our fight to say "Enough!" to addictive patterns means learning about and understanding these things. Wise people are in a position to show us what is and what is not gold. It is worthwhile investigating what wise people say and do.

Some Gold Nuggets

Here are some of the gold nuggets found by wise people:

1 They try to have a good motivation for whatever they do.

Man is here for the sake of other men—above all for those upon whose smile and well-being our own happiness depends, and also for the countless unknown souls with whose fate we are connected by a bond of sympathy. —ALBERT EINSTEIN[27]

Even if things don't turn out the way we want, at least we know we are trying. What is a good motivation? Anything which helps other people, birds, animals, insects, and so on. If we need to keep to ourselves for a while, then we can do that so we have time to clear our minds. That way we develop our own little wisdoms and will be less likely to harm ourselves or others. We might be able to give a little happiness or relief from suffering to someone who needs it. We are following this wisdom each time we choose our motivation for a meditation.

2 They try not to give in to the urge for immediate gratification.

If you're going through hell, keep going.
—WINSTON CHURCHILL[28]

This might feel like giving up all pleasure and happiness, but in fact we put ourselves in a position for better quality pleasure and happiness. Lama Zopa Rinpoche says that "hundreds of problems come from dissatisfaction." This is because we are dissatisfied when we do not get what we want or desire. "When there is very strong desire, it is very easy to become angry, for example. The stronger the clinging, the stronger the anger that arises." You feel completely trapped and suffocated. "If you don't cling very much, you don't get so angry when someone upsets you. You might still be disturbed, but less than before."[29]

Letting go of the urge for immediate gratification, even deliberately making the effort not to indulge, loosens up the addiction trap. We have set in motion a new way of doing things and if we keep this new way, then we have begun to establish a new and positive habit. What seems so hard comes from the dissatisfaction that arises when we cannot indulge in our addiction. At those times we are forced to face the pain behind the addiction, the pain of withdrawal. But if we can hang in there and be honest about that pain, then we find more gold nuggets, more little wisdoms.

3 They realize that life is too short to spend it being miserable, angry, depressed, jealous, and so on.

As an atheist, I believe that all life is unspeakably precious, because it's only here for a brief moment, a flare against the dark, and then it's gone forever. — JOSEPH MICHAEL STRACZYNSKI[30]

It's much better to investigate why we feel these miserable states and do something about them. In particular, we need to see how we ourselves generate these states. They do not come from other people or outside events. In any case, the things which we want so desperately we have to leave behind when we die. The only thing we take with us is our mind or soul. We might as well make sure that this mind or soul is in a good position for a positive life after death.

Since we don't know when we are going to die, it makes sense to be prepared now. Jesus said, "Keep watch because you do not know the day or the hour your Lord will come."[31] We need to do something to make our lives meaningful.

4 They develop useful, positive habits.

The tree bears fruit after its kind both in the soil and in the soul. If we spend the time we waste in sighing for the perfect golden fruit in fulfilling

the conditions of its growth, happiness will come, must come. It is guaran-
teed in the very laws of the universe. —HELEN KELLER[32]

Pride, anger, jealousy, and depression happen when we let go of
control over our mind and assume that we are more important than
anyone else. One of the most important positive habits to develop is
the thought that all these negative emotions come from one's own
mind, from our egos. We want to always be important, or wealthy,
or comfortable, or loved by everyone; we get upset when this does
not happen. If we give up those motivations, we can relax.

We already know that habits can be good and useful. When
we try to change our destructive behavior into positive behavior,
it seems hard at first. It is hard because we are undermining an
ingrained habit. The more we can ingrain the positive habit, the less
likely we are to fall into the old habit.

Instead of trying to be important, we can try to do the best we
can. Instead of anxiously waiting for lots of money, we can learn
to be satisfied with what we have. Instead of getting upset with
the least bit of discomfort, we can learn to tolerate it for the time
being. Instead of wanting everyone to love us, we can learn to love
everyone else.

5 They recognize the ego for what it is, a mere story that they have made up about themselves.

Men do change, and change comes like a little wind that ruffles the
curtains at dawn, and it comes like the stealthy perfume of wildflowers
hidden in the grass. —JOHN STEINBECK[33]

We live in a hallucination. My ego is a story I have made up for
myself, but the story seems real. But since it is just a story, then each
of us can make up a new story. Which story is real? None of them,
but some stories are more effective than others. If my story is that
I am a victim, then it is only a story. It may be based on things that
did happen, but that does not mean that I have to believe that I am
always a victim.

Understanding the ego as a story means that I can be open

to change. My external circumstances are always changing. I can change my story. Nothing is fixed.

6 They cherish others as much as, or more than, they cherished themselves.

The sole meaning of life is to serve humanity. —LEO TOLSTOY[34]

When we are addicted, we are totally focused on ourselves and our own needs. What would happen if, instead, we became as focused on the needs of other people? For a start, we would not have enough space in our minds to even think about our addiction. Lama Zopa puts it well: "When you are cherishing yourself, thinking only of yourself—'How can I be happy? How can I be free of problems?'—there is no happiness in your heart, only worry and fear. You see only problems, and your mind is not relaxed. But in the next moment, when you change your object of concern to another sentient being . . . suddenly your heart is released from self-cherishing, like limbs released from chains . . . there is suddenly peace in the very depths of your heart. Right in the very moment that your mind changes from self-cherishing to cherishing others, there is liberation, freedom from the tight bondage of the selfish mind."[35]

7 They understand how difficulties like addictions are opportunities, not overwhelming obstacles.

He who learns must suffer
And even in our sleep pain that cannot forget
Falls drop by drop upon the heart,
And in our own despite, against our will,
Comes wisdom to us by the awful grace of God. —AESCHYLUS[36]

As we work on the suffering we experience as a result of the addiction, then we acquire skills that otherwise we probably would not develop. We become wiser and more considerate of others. Our relationships with people improve and we begin to feel a connectedness with others that we had been missing. We develop a natural wish to benefit others instead of harming them, which also means that we look for effective ways to do this.

When our addictions have developed through our reactions to others being selfish and not recognizing the suffering they have been causing, we begin to see that without these enemies, we would not have the same opportunity to develop all this compassionate wisdom. This means that our "enemies" have actually been excellent teachers, even though that is probably not what they intended. It may seem crazy to say "Thank you" to an enemy, but if we can see how we have benefited, then it may be possible. This is also the mind behind forgiveness.

Our Addiction Is Part of the Solution

If you are feeling bewildered by the gap between your wisdom and that of a wise person, there is no need for despair. We become wise through working our way through problems. Wisdom does not come just from reading books, but from experiencing life and all its difficulties. Wisdom comes from being in the thick of problems and working our way through them with humility and courage, which in turn arise from honesty and equanimity.

The addiction itself is the most powerful tool for destroying addiction. Why? Because the suffering we experience as a result of the addiction is the most powerful motivator for getting out of it.

In the end we are all addicted in some way. The most powerful and subtle addiction is our addiction to seeing ourselves as something solid, always the same, existing as if it has some material reality. In fact, as Buddhism teaches, the way we see ourselves is just something we have created from our own mind. We can see ourselves differently just by choosing to do so. When we understand this, we can choose. We can take responsibility for who we are.

Remember Jake from Chapter 4? He has a typical chocolate and junk food addiction and is overweight. He even likes watching those TV programs about people losing weight. He feels superior because he is not as bad as they are. He eats his chocolate as he watches. He prefers his comfort to the hard work of losing weight.

If you ask him to describe himself he says, "I've got my act together. I like myself this way. This is the way I've always been: friend to everyone, friend to myself, laid back. Easy come, easy go."

One day his doctor says, "Do you know you will die soon? You've got serious heart problems and serious diabetes. If your heart doesn't give up on you, then the diabetes will get to you. You know, ulcerated legs, blindness. Do you want to die soon?"

There's nothing like the threat of death to give us a shock. Jake does not want to die, but if he is going to set himself up for a longer life, he needs to do something different. Most importantly, he needs to change the way he sees himself. Firstly, he has to admit that he doesn't have his act together. If he did, he would not be overweight. Will he realize this or not? Secondly, he has to see that being laid back is not always good. This means he has to see himself as someone who can take control, who can be determined. Will he do this? We don't know, but we do know that if he doesn't change his view of himself and then change his way of doing things, then he will die within a year or two.

So let's say that Jake does make these changes. He chooses to see himself differently: as being determined, as taking control of his life, as being able to follow through on decisions. He now describes himself differently because he has been shocked into seeing himself differently. In particular, as he loses weight, he also begins to feel much better about himself than he did before. He even begins to see that feeling complacent was a poor sort of happiness. And because he is an armchair philosopher, he suddenly sees that there is a new form of happiness which has come about from doing things which were uncomfortable. There is a new form of confidence which comes from being able to tolerate the discomfort and to wait for the benefits.

But Jake also finds an unexpected bonus. He knows from first-hand experience just how devastating it is to be grossly overweight. He decides to help other people with the same problem. He finds that by sharing his story with other people who share their stories: they become connected. This connectedness with other people Jake finds deeply satisfying. There is no way he would now give up this deep happiness for the pseudohappiness of being a couch potato.

He realizes that this deep happiness has paradoxically come about through his addiction, not so much his addiction to chocolate, but his addiction to seeing himself in a certain way.

Buddhism teaches just this: the usual way in which we see ourselves is a fantasy, a delusion. We don't have to be deluded. We don't have to see ourselves in a fixed way. When we realize that, then we are open to change simply because we now know that change is possible.

what is the point in saying "enough!"?

8

[Spiritual] practice doesn't just mean sitting on the meditation cushion—
it has everything to do with the practicality of living and working with
your negative states of mind, with lessening them, counteracting them when
they arise, and ensuring that, once subdued, they do not arise again.
Thus it is very important that your [spiritual] training should also entail
you actively engaging with society. It is not only a matter of cultivating
positive thoughts, or fostering goodness and kindness in your attitude.
For every meditation session that you do on cultivating the altruistic mind,
you should allocate an equal amount of time in the post-meditation period
to the practical engagement of that mind.
—Yangsi Rinpoche[37]

THERE IS NO point in saying "Enough!" to addiction if we do not make an effort to change our lives. What is the point in being healthy if we simply repeat the old patterns and become ill or unhappy again? If our lives are simply boring or meaningless, then we might as well stay with the addiction. At least we would then have some occasional pleasure. Of course most of us want something more. By the time we have thought about and meditated on the ideas in the previous chapters, we have developed enough wisdom to know that we are looking for more than occasional pleasure. We will want to know how to find this deeper satisfaction that is connected with lasting happiness.

Some of us are desperately lonely. Some of us are so traumatized by the people who should have loved us that we feel completely shut off, disconnected. It is not surprising that in these cases we might react with bitterness, or resentment, or anger, or hopelessness when such things happen. Even suicide might seem like a solution. If feelings like these become habitual, we begin to react in the same way to all other people, whether they deserve this or not. We become like a frightened child cowering in a corner and afraid of everybody, even when someone genuinely offers love and support. Since feeling unlovable and being unable to love are probably the deepest emotional pain we suffer, then obviously learning to love and to be lovable in return is an important step towards better quality happiness.

It is one thing to stop the habit itself. It is another thing to choose the changes and develop the tools which make an addiction unnecessary. The moment we make the choice to hold our hand out to be helped or to help others, we have at the same time changed our values. We have decided that kindness, courage, and hope are values worth having. These are the sorts of values which reconnect us with people. They are found in the great religions, but they are not necessarily religious values. They are the values which unite everybody. More importantly, these are the values which restore a deep and satisfying happiness.

Freedom from the Isolation of an Addiction: Tools for Reconnecting

When we say "Enough!" to addiction then we are also saying that we want to be reconnected. We want warmth and affection and laughter and a deep satisfaction in our lives. Forgiveness is one tool for reconnecting, whether we forgive anyone who has harmed us or we receive forgiveness from people we have harmed. We may think, "Well why bother making the effort to reconnect?" The answer is that this is where deeper happiness lies. As His Holiness the Dalai Lama says, the meaning of life is simple: it is to cherish others.

The after-addiction future, then, is about reconnecting, not just with people but also with our external world, the environment, and the energies of pure compassionate wisdom that come from our religious and spiritual awareness. To get there, we need to check out our values. We all have values, for better or worse, as we will see in Chapter 9. There is no point in a value system that makes us unhappy. The values we want are simply rules for living happy, effective lives. A happy and effective life necessarily means reconnecting with everything around us: our environment, our sense of the spiritual life, and especially other people.

Of course, equanimity is our key tool. Even after we decide to change, we will sometimes find ourselves repeating old patterns. Other people may not recognize our efforts, as Carri in Chapter 7 found in one version of her story.

For a start it helps to be honest about the values that we actually use, as distinct from the ones we know we ought to use. For example, if I am in a paranoid state and believe that everyone is out to get me, then I would want to protect myself and fight off the enemy. I would then value being cunning and devious and getting rid of my enemies as quickly as possible. If I was in a clinging state, my values might be about being manipulative. In addiction, my value system is simple: anything to run away from reality.

While we are in the grip of an addiction, our values are related to getting what we want as soon as we want it. We begin to value deceit, stealing, bad-mouthing people who are trying to help us, and feeling angry towards them. We might even feel like killing to get what we want, or abusing people sexually. These things are listed in the ten nonvirtues taught in Buddhism.[38] They are the values that harm others and us as well.

Angulimala was a murderer who lived at the time of the Buddha. He believed that he could become enlightened by killing a hundred people. So he valued whatever helped him to do this: speed, stealth, strength, and a very sharp knife. He would chop off one finger from each of his victims and hang the finger on a string around his neck so he could keep count of them. The story opens when he has ninety-nine fingers and needs just one more. He comes across Shakyamuni Buddha and tries to kill him. The Buddha is cleverer than Angulimala and could not be caught. When Angulimala was exhausted, the Buddha sat down with him and began to talk. He was able to point out that Angulimala's philosophy was faulty and taught Angulimala a new philosophy. Angulimala saw the sense of the Buddha's teaching. Now he had a new set of values. He probably still valued speed and strength and sharp knives, but for very different reasons, perhaps for harvesting crops, and he started to value new qualities, such as kindness and patience and generosity. This was not the end of the story—Angulimala had to put up with the villagers not believing he had changed. They were still terrified of him. Ridding ourselves of bad habits does not necessarily mean living in a rosy world afterwards.

From the story of Angulimala we can see that the values we hold are the ones that support our beliefs about what will make us happy. If we believe that by being kind and helping to remove any suffering we can be happy, then our values will be the tools we use to support that philosophy.

As we emerge from our addictions, we begin to see the faults in our old values, and we can start to look for a new set of tools for our new value system. We are going to look at what positive tools we can develop to fill in the gap. These positive tools are called values and their basis is ethics. There are many ways of listing the values that go with a philosophy of loving-kindness towards ourselves and others. There are the Ten Commandments, to which Jesus Christ added a new one with a positive value: "Love one another as I have loved you."[39] There is the eightfold path of Buddhism.[40] It is framed in terms of "right": that is, right understanding, right thought, right speech, and so on. We determine what is "right" through our wisdom knowledge. The values which bring us happiness are based on the same wisdom knowledge. The ten virtues of Buddhism of course are the opposite of the nonvirtues: not being deceitful, not stealing, not bad-mouthing, and so on.

Ethics are simply the values for living happy, effective lives. What we think and do affect people around us. What we do is a reflection of what we believe about ourselves and others. If we believe that we want to be happy, then we find ways to be happy. We are not going to be happy if everyone around us is miserable. So it makes sense to find ways for other people to be happy as well. We have begun to realize that there is a connection between our own happiness and their happiness. If there is such a connection, then we need to know how to make it a life-affirming connection rather than a harmful connection.

Here we are going to do this by looking at the "Sixteen Guidelines for Life." These sixteen guidelines have been adapted by the Foundation for Developing Compassion and Wisdom from a poem written by a seventh-century Tibetan, King Songtsen Gampo.[41] When we read through them, it becomes obvious that these guidelines refer to life-affirming universal values. They are divided into four sections with four guidelines in each section. The first section is about how we think and introduces the values of humility, patience, contentment, and delight as tools for reconnecting with ourselves and our world. The second section introduces ways we can act which support the process of reconnecting: kindness, honesty, gentleness, and right speech. The third section introduces ways in which we can interact with compassionate wisdom: respect, forgiveness, gratitude, and loyalty. Finally, we meet the tools which help us to find meaning in our lives: principles, aspiration, service, and courage.

Values and Happiness:
The Sixteen Guidelines for a Happy Life

Each of the sixteen guidelines can be a meditation in itself. We can choose to follow them one by one, or we can choose one of them to think about and take to heart. We can spend a small amount of time reading just one of the sixteen qualities or we can meditate on that one guideline for many weeks. There is no single approach that suits everyone. It is up to each of us to decide.

When we choose to meditate on one of the sixteen guidelines, then it helps to remember to reflect on our motivation for doing the meditation, to find a way to tune in to compassionate wisdom, to take time to recall and be happy about the benefits of our meditation, and finally to dedicate our meditation at the close of each session. Each of us is free to do this in our own way. Those of us using the book in a group might choose to select one group member to create and lead a motivation and dedication for each guideline

Tools for How We Think:
Humility, Patience, Contentment, Delight

Although we can work to remove the negative thoughts related to addiction, life would be boring if we had no positive thoughts and emotions to replace the negative ones. These emotions may seem impossible to feel after we have spent most of our lives being addicted and under the power of the negative thoughts that go with addiction. We need to remind ourselves of some of the wisdom we have been gathering from this book and from other sources. The mind can change. I can change.

We are now trying to develop new habits. A habit forms when we do something often, and when we have a strong motivation to create the habit. This means that we need to try out these new ways of thinking as often as we can, even if they seem awkward at first. The motivation is to remove the addiction habit. We can make that motivation even stronger when we realize that we can rejoin the human race. And we can add more strength to the motivation if we strongly and sincerely decide to do this to help people who are suffering. We develop this familiarity when we meditate by remembering the new way of being over and over again.

Imagine what your life would be like if you used the tools of a generous mind—humility, patience, contentment, and delight. Instead of the acid of bitterness, we start to become connected to ourselves and connected to others in a way that brings lightness and happiness. Who would want to be addicted when such lightness and happiness are possible?

Humility

Humility is one of the secrets of wise people such as His Holiness the Dalai Lama, Mother Teresa, Nelson Mandela, St. Francis of Assisi, and Mahatma Gandhi. Humility comes from knowing clearly where we stand and not trying to pretend to be different. It comes from having equanimity towards ourselves. People with humility can see beyond their own viewpoint and interests. They are open to other viewpoints. Humility shifts our perspective from "me" to "others." What would happen if Duncan practiced humility? He would find it very hard at first, but even the first small efforts would mean that his relationships at home and at work would begin to change. How would your own life be different if you made a deliberate attempt to be humble?

Patience

Patience means not flaring up when someone disagrees with us or wants to hurt us, or when things go wrong. It is the opposite of instant gratification. If we try to practice patience, at first we might just become a block of wood and this would give us the space to apply equanimity. In particular, we need to practice patience towards times of relapse. If we remind ourselves that it takes time to undo the habit and to loosen the hold of triggers, then we can be patient. Patience can also reduce conflict between us and others because it reduces the need to strike back. Instead of conflict, we find ourselves being kind and respectful. People begin to see us and relate to us differently. It might help to learn the great prayer about patience: "Lord, help me to accept the things I cannot change, the courage to change the things I can change, and the wisdom to know the difference."

Contentment

Contentment is about being satisfied with what we have instead of always wanting more. Someone who is deeply contented has no need to hurt another or to profit at another person's expense. People with addictions are discontented people. We are discontented when we cannot get access to whatever we are addicted to. We are discontented even while indulging in our addictive behavior because we know it is not going to last forever. Contentment is not the same as not caring about anything. Can you imagine a contented person and compare that with a person who does not care? Thinking about the differences between the two gives us clues as to what contentment is about. Can you imagine what your life would be like if you were always contented? There would be no strain or stress even when you do not get what you might want.

Delight

Delight is missing from the heart of an addicted person. It has been replaced by the excitement, or the numbness, of addiction. Delight comes about when we have love, contentment, and humility in our hearts. It is a sheer joy in the world and the people around us. How can we develop a habit of delight?

We make delight a tool when we begin to notice little things. We can take delight in the flowering of a neglected plant, or in the sounds of birds, or the smile of a small child. We can take delight in our efforts to break our addiction, even the tiny successes. Making a deliberate effort to be joyful might seem artificial at first, but it breaks our mind away from its usual negativity. This wise openness of delight melts away envy, resentment, arrogance, meanness, and so on. We might even cultivate delight to such an extent that we can genuinely rejoice when someone gets something that we had wanted for ourselves. Our own misery melts away and we feel happy regardless of our circumstances. Can you imagine your heart filled with delight? What differences would this make in your life?

Tools for How We Act:
Kindness, Honesty, Generosity, Right Speech

Reconnecting with others means that the way we behave becomes important. We cannot reconnect if we are full of pride, arrogance, bitterness, jealousy, depression, resentment, and the behavior that goes with these emotions. So now we will look at new ways of acting to replace old and ineffective methods which might have come about through the self-centeredness of our addictions. How we act is about living out the values which help us have better relationships with others.

Kindness

Kindness says, "I want you to be happy." We are more inclined to think about what we have done for ourselves than about what other people have done for us. We even fall into the trap of believing that no one is ever kind to us, so why should we be kind to them? Yet, wherever we are and whatever we are doing, we depend on countless kind acts from other people. My lunch , even if I put it together myself, is still made from food that has come through the kindness of others. There are the people who sold me the food, the people who transported it to the shops, the people who grew the food, and the people who have cared for all the people we have just mentioned. Even if you grew everything in your lunch yourself, where did the seeds come from? Who taught you how to garden? Who constructed the stove, or the chopping board, or the road to your house, or your clothes, and so on. When we begin to think in this way, we begin to see how we are always dependent on other people, and they too are dependent on us. These little acts of kindness from others are the positive aspects of the interdependency of all of us on this earth. Remembering this, our hearts feel just that little bit warmer.

If a small act of kindness can help us to open our hearts and help the hearts of others to be open, that would be better for the whole world. There would be no bullying or wars or greed. As His Holiness the Dalai Lama says, cultivating a close warmhearted feeling for others automatically puts our mind at ease.

Can you imagine yourself always being kind? Can you feel an openness in your heart when you think about this? Is there one small act of kindness that you can do today?

Honesty

Honesty is a tough one for people who have been stealing to get enough money for their addiction. Most of us have denied for years that we have an addiction, both to ourselves and to people who have tried to point out the truth to us. Actually, it is tough for all of us. The impulse to get more, or to protect ourselves from an ugly truth, is very strong. There are the many little ways in which we do not practice honesty. Even eating more than our fair share of food is a lack of integrity. We might be very quick to point out if we have been overcharged, but very slow to point out if we have been undercharged. When everyone lacks honesty, then no one can be trusted. We would live in a dangerous world of chronic suspicion, and that would lead to more conflict.

Wise people are known to be honest. They can be trusted. There is no need to be paranoid in their presence. The honesty of wise people is mixed with an equanimity which does not set one person above or below another when it comes to human needs. If the whole world could be wise in this way, then we would trust each other. We would share what we have without resentment. There would be no wars.

Can you imagine yourself always being honest? What difference would it make to the people you relate to? Is there one small act of honesty you can do today?

Generosity

Generosity is not just giving money to a good cause. Even if we have no money, we can be generous by having a kind heart. Smiling at people we pass in the street is the generosity of kindness, or just having the thought that this person should be free of pain. Putting out water for the birds or putting our food waste back in the garden is an act of generosity. If every one of us could make a greater effort to reduce our energy consumption, it would have a definite impact on the pollution, global warming, and extreme geological and climatic events that are causing so much suffering around the world.

Here is a Sufi story:

> There were once two brothers who jointly farmed a field, and always shared its yield.
>
> One day, one of them woke up in the night and thought: "My brother is married and has children. Because of this he has anxieties and expenses which are not mine. So I will go and move some sacks from my storeroom, which is only fair. I shall do this under cover of night, so that he may not, from his generosity, dispute with me about it."
>
> He moved the sacks and went back to bed.
>
> Soon after the other brother woke up and thought to himself: "It is not fair that I should have half the corn in our field. My brother, who is unmarried, lacks my pleasures in having a family, so I will therefore try to compensate a little by moving some of my corn into his storeroom."
>
> So saying, he did so.
>
> The next morning, each was amazed that he still had the same number of sacks in his storeroom, and afterwards neither could understand why year after year, the number of sack remained the same even when each of them shifted some by stealth.[42]

If we make a deliberate decision to help others as much as we can, then that decision in itself breaks up the intense self-focus of an addiction. We are wasting time when our minds are clouded by the addiction itself.

Generosity is different for different people. It depends more on the motivation for giving than on the gift itself. For one person, donating five dollars to charity is a huge act of generosity. For another, that five dollar donation is nothing, barely noticed. If we are going to practice generosity, then our motivation needs to be focused on the needs of the person we are giving to rather than being focused on our own pride and grandeur.

What acts of generosity can you make at this point in your life?

What can you offer to others? It may be something small like giving up your seat on the bus. However small, if it is made with a wise motivation, it will open and warm your heart.

Right Speech

Speech that is not harmful is the meaning of "right speech." It is wise speech. Wise people can still be quite firm and decisive when that is what is needed. It means finding generous and productive ways of saying things. There are times when we need to be strict, but we do not have to denigrate or harm the person or child who is out of line. Firm speech can also be wise speech.

Wise speech is another tool that can be practiced. We can begin by practicing wise speech to ourselves—replacing the inner voice of guilt that is putting us down and opening a space to listen to our deeper needs.

What can I say which will be helpful to someone? What tone of voice will I use? And when is it wise to say nothing? Imagine yourself actually saying something helpful and supportive. Imagine the difference it would make in your life if you could say just one helpful thing to one person. Imagine your life if your speech always came from wisdom. This is another tool that Duncan could well use.

Tools for How We Relate to Others: Respect, Forgiveness, Gratitude, Loyalty

There are plenty of teenagers like Kurt. He is into a Gothic phase. He wears mostly black, has pierced various parts of his body, and likes it if people look a little scared of him. So one day I asked him if that was what he really wanted. In a way, he did, but he also realized that he didn't want everyone to be scared of him. He still wanted friends, and a family who believed in him. He still wanted to be taken seriously by his teachers. He still wears Gothic, but at least he has cut his hair so that it does not hide his eyes. His Gothic phase is his way of asking for respect, but he has not yet fully thought through how his clothes affect other people in his life. In this section we look at the values we adopt so that we can relate to others with compassionate wisdom.

Respect: Giving Respect and Being Respected

We give respect to people we like and admire, and sometimes also a guarded respect to people we fear. When we respect someone we acknowledge their kindness to us and sometimes we take them as a role model. The role model is someone that already has everything we want, even if what we want has been created by the advertising industry. We emulate a role model because we want to be happy and the role model appears to be happy. Advertisers use role models all the time.

Some role models show us how to have a life full of meaning and connectedness. Other role models show us how to be ruthless, or self-indulgent, or superficial, anything so long as we get what we want. It can be quite interesting to look back on the various role models we had in the past. It gives us some insight into who we are now.

If we want to break our addiction trap, then it is useful to have as role models people who have been through the same difficulties. This is one of the reasons why a self-help group like Alcoholics Anonymous can be so successful. In a group like that we meet people who have suffered as much or even more than we have but still are managing to get their lives back together. How do they do it? By using these people as role models we find some answers for ourselves.

If copying a role model means that I can be like that role model, then it makes sense to take on role models using our wisdom mind. If I want to dress for a job interview, who would be a good role model? If I want my children to be happy, who would be a good role model? If I want to speak out confidently, who would be a good role model? If I want a deep sense of satisfaction in my life, who would be a good role model? Jean-Claude Killy, a French Alpine skier, said that the best and fastest way to learn a sport is to watch and imitate a champion.[43]

We can look to role models who already live with kindness, forgiveness, humility, joy, gentle speech, moderation, integrity, and fidelity. Who are these people? Often they have a religious background: His Holiness the Dalai Lama, Nelson Mandela, Mahatma Gandhi, and Martin Luther King. They come from all races and any religion teaching great wisdom and profound compassion. These are the people who show us, through their own lives, that we also can be like that, that we also can generate these positive qualities. And what about the great role models: Moses, Shakyamuni Buddha, Jesus Christ, the prophet Muhammad? These people have preached those qualities we are looking for and changed whole nations .

On the other hand, we are role models too, for better or worse. Have you stopped to think how kids might think about you? What sort of image do they get of you? Do you let them see it all or do you hide the parts you are ashamed of? If they are going to copy you, what sort of people will they turn out to be?

What does respect mean to a wise person? The wise person respects all living things without exception. That respect comes from equanimity. It does not mean that the wise person idolizes everyone but rather she or he can see the struggle for happiness that we all have. When we respect each other in this way, then we encourage any thought or behavior that helps another person's struggle for lasting and satisfying happiness.

Can you imagine yourself respecting someone you dislike or despise? What would this mean? How would this change the way you relate to this person? Imagine yourself with the tool of respect so deeply ingrained that you automatically respect everyone.

Forgiveness:
Especially to People Who Have Harmed Us

Parents are often targeted as the cause of psychological problems, and of course no parents are perfect. "I was put down so much. I felt so bad all the time," or "They drank so I drank too and when I drank I felt better. So my parents are to blame for my alcoholism." Even if we can justifiably blame them as contributing to our addiction, that does not mean they did nothing at all for us.

Even if your parents were failures as parents, then you still have lots to be thankful for. As a baby you were totally helpless. Somehow you have got to the point where you are able to read this book. The people who fed you, wiped your bottom, and cleaned up your vomit deserve some thanks. As we turn our minds towards the positive things our parents and other people have done for us, and with forgiveness towards the rest, then we have the possibility of relating to them with kindness and forgiveness and generosity of spirit. We do this with our wisdom mind.

Mostly parents try to do the right thing by their children, but unfortunately parents are not perfect and even if they were, kids have their own minds. One child in an alcoholic family will decide never to touch the stuff. Another child might think, "If you can't beat them, join them." One might decide it is all too much and just give up on them and on the rest of the world. Another child might decide to try to fix the problem by finding the bottles and pouring the alcohol down the sink. However bad your parents might have been, you can choose how you will deal with that.

Why would someone be a bad parent? It may be because they don't know much about children. Why not? Maybe their own parents didn't know how to handle kids. It may be because they were caught up in their own addictions. Why? Perhaps that was the only solution they had to a painful life. Maybe they just don't know how to love. Why? Because they were never loved themselves.

When we think like this, with a mind of equanimity towards our parents' mistakes, then we can see that they also were unhappy, that they also didn't have better ways of dealing with problems and pain. This is how the mind of forgiveness can arise. Forgiveness does not say that it did not matter. Forgiveness sees that the mistakes came from pain and ignorance.

As a child, even if we are now an adult child, we can acknowledge and honor the beneficial things our parents have done. This is part of forgiveness. Bringing harmony into a disharmonious family situation can be one of the biggest challenges we face in life.

In the Ten Commandments we are told to honor our father and mother. In Tibetan Buddhism, the path to generating compassion is based on honoring the kindness of our mothers. When we accept that we exist thanks to our parents, then it would seem a bit unbalanced if we were not able to express our gratitude and appreciation to them. Sincere gratitude is a warm feeling that melts away tension. It can support the psychological health and happiness both of ourselves and of the person being affirmed.

Parents are not the only people who betray our trust or hurt us in some way. Forgiving such people does not mean that their actions were acceptable. It means that we begin to see that they were out of control because of their own suffering, that they needed help just as we do.

Gratitude

It often seems that there is nothing we can be grateful for, especially if we have had a tough life. If we stop to look more carefully, then we find many things which have been good, even if they are very small things. We cannot eat unless there is food. This means that we are dependent on the farmers and truck drivers, and people who package the food, and more truck drivers or sailors or pilots who deliver the food to the shops and then the shopkeepers and assistants and the boy who gathers the shopping carts. If we take it home in the car, then there are the people who mine the materials and manufacture the car and the truckers who take it to the car dealership to sell and the many people who manufacture and supply the gas for the gas station, and so on. Once we are home, then there are builders and more manufacturers and workmen who built the place in which we live. This is part of the long list of people who had a part in making our food accessible.

When we think like this about the countless ways in which people have benefited—and so been kind to—us, we begin to feel as if we are standing at the top of a huge pyramid. The only purpose of this pyramid is to support us. We are all part of this huge interdependent network of supporting and being supported.

Wherever each of us happens to be at this moment, we can think about all the people who have had a hand in bringing our environment together. Even having this book to read has come about through the interdependence of many people. I may have written it, but my ideas have been formed by my teachers and their teachers going back in a long lineage. I would not even be here if it were not for the kindness of my parents. There are the people who have helped me by reading early drafts, my editor, the people who print the book, the people who deliver it, the people who have brought the bookshop together, and so on.

If we take time to reflect in this way on a regular basis, we begin to feel how the human race fits together, supporting each other with a greater or lesser degree of skillfulness. Our sense of gratitude becomes boundless and our feeling of loneliness evaporates into nothing.

Loyalty

After meditating on gratitude, we begin to realize how we are interconnected with everyone, not just with our friends and family. If we are interconnected, then we might as well do our best to make these interconnections as life-giving as possible.

Loyalty is concerned with the future of our relationships. It is about hanging in there with our friends and family even when they are in trouble, even when they hurt us. Loyalty means that we can be trusted to keep our word. It means that what we say is truthful and supportive. Politicians are fond of reminding us that we should be loyal to our nation. What they mean is that we should support our fellow countrymen rather than the countrymen of another nation. But loyalty does not have to be exclusive or racist. We can be loyal to all people and races on this planet. Loyalty is also applied to sexual and family relationships. Shakespeare's *Romeo and Juliet* is about the foolishness and harm of misplaced loyalty. Clearly we need to find out what loyalty means to wise people.

Disloyalty and infidelity are words often applied to sexual relationships. They are used when one partner cheats on the other one, but if you think about it, you will see that they apply to all relationships. If we experience disloyalty, then we might use it as an excuse for bitterness, revenge, arrogance, self-loathing, depression, or jealousy. We might excuse our own unfaithfulness by blaming our partner for being at fault. Then we feel we have a righteous justification for arrogance, greed, and chronic dissatisfaction. We do not have to react in such a negative way. We could instead see that our disloyal partner or parent or friend is under the influence of his or her own pain and find compassion in our hearts.

Loyalty builds trust. A baby learns to trust that its mother is going to feed it, change its diapers, keep it warm but not too warm, find a soft place for it to sleep, and so on. When these things happen, then it feels safe. Mom, Dad, the whole world can be trusted. It is the loyalty of Mom and Dad which helps the baby to feel safe and loved. When we do not get it, especially as babies, then we become suspicious and stop trusting people.

Loyalty can be twisted and misused. Let's go back to Duncan at his worst. He is married and intends staying married because that proves he is a good guy. His wife has to look good all the time. His kids have to be best at everything. His wife is supposed to agree to everything he says and if she does not agree, then she is being disloyal. Duncan is not concerned with how his wife feels or what is important to her. He is not concerned with integrity, but with his image. He uses the word "loyalty" to make his wife prop up this image. When we think about Duncan, we begin to see again how loyalty needs the wisdom of integrity as one of its qualities.

What about loyalty towards ourselves? If I am being disloyal to myself, I am letting myself down, I am undermining the best parts of myself. It means that I don't care about myself. If I don't care about myself, then I don't care about others either. It doesn't matter what they think. I'll just get what I can for myself and they can go to hell. My life is nothing so I'll get what I can and damn the consequences. So what if I'm addicted? At least I get a few moments of happiness. And so we progressively destroy our lives and, with it, other lives are destroyed. Loyalty to ourselves means staying with our efforts to make wise changes.

One way of meditating on loyalty is to examine our own minds for moments when we have been loyal and moments when we have been disloyal. Why did we act in this way? What were the effects on the people to whom we were loyal or disloyal? What is it that stops me from being loyal?

Although values such as integrity and loyalty may seem artificial at first sight, as we apply wisdom to thinking about them we come to see that they are essential for our happiness. We also begin to see the value of kindness, forgiveness, and humility, of gentle speech and balance. As we begin to put these things together, then our relationships improve, we feel happier, the need for the addiction loosens and maybe even drops away.

Tools for Finding Meaning: Principles, Aspiration, Service, Courage

When our life has meaning, then it is also satisfying. Sometimes addictions are ways of escaping from a life that seems to be going nowhere and has nothing to offer. Running away through our addictions does not solve the problem. The question then is: how do we find meaning in life?

Principles

Our principles arise from what we value. They are rules for putting our values into practice in our daily lives. Often there can be a difference between the principles we say we hold and what we actually do. That is hypocrisy. It also means that our minds are divided. The angel and the devil often argue and the devil wins out. The angel argues that you will be in a big mess if you go for your addiction. The devil argues that you will be in a big mess if you don't.

Then there are people who hold principles that create harm and bigotry. The principle of the Nazi era was that the German race was superior and therefore it was legitimate to wipe out inferior races.

For them, the meaning of life is limited to some people and other people are of no value. This is also a principle of terrorism.

Perhaps it's the lack of clear positive principles that makes our lives so challenging and complicated. Principles are like the spokes that hold a bicycle wheel together. They can provide a set of values that will help us make key decisions and underpin our thoughts, speech, and actions. In times of difficulty, when we may not be able to think clearly, it can be enormously helpful to be guided by a set of personal principles.

The principles we need for kindness to pervade our planet and its nations are very simple. At the very least the principle is not to hurt another being. At its peak the principle is to bring happiness to every being. All the other ethical principles are based on these.

So if I stop to look at my addiction, what are the principles on which it is based? Are these really the principles I want for my happiness? Do I agree in theory that ethical principles are important but in practice live out selfish principles? As we try to answer these questions for ourselves, we are developing our wisdom mind. Then we need to plant that wisdom mind firmly. We do that through daily practice. Then we need to act according to our wisdom.

When we feel that life has no meaning, then it seems pointless to continue living. Why not commit suicide? It would seem to save a lot of effort. Addictions provide a temporary relief from this painful emotional state. The addictive habit in itself can be a distraction from that sense of meaninglessness.

Would you be caught in your addiction if your life had meaning? Would your addiction be important if there was something even more urgent in your life? When we have meaning in our lives, we are inspired. We don't need an addictive hit to give us energy. To be inspired means, literally, to take a deep breath in.

Inspiration and Aspiration

What inspires us? Surely it is when we hear of or meet people who have achieved things that we would like to achieve, especially when their achievement has come through a lot of courage and persistence. We begin to think that our dreams really are possible. Helen Keller, who was born blind and deaf, became an inspiration not only to other blind and deaf children, but to anyone who read her story. She said in an essay on optimism that although the world is full of suffering, it is also full of the overcoming of it.

Then there is the story of an Australian, Fred Hollows, who found the money and time to travel to Third World countries to remove cataracts and reverse that form of blindness in countless numbers of poor people. He says, in a TV ad asking for donations, that each person is as worthy of his care and attention to detail as the Prime Minister of Australia. How wonderful that anyone should have such kindness to others. How wonderful also because it means that I, too, have the possibility of being so kind.

There are the stories of the saints and prophets and bodhisattvas. The great yogi Milarepa would have been at home with the worst of our punk gangs when he was a teenager. He practiced black magic and managed to kill a lot of people. Then he heard about someone whose magic was even better than his, Marpa. He went to get teachings from Marpa, who at first would have nothing to do with him. Milarepa used all sorts of tricks to get teachings, and what he got was a healthy dose of Buddhism. Milarepa became disgusted with his past. Eventually he went to meditate in a cave. He ate only nettles and his skin turned green. He had no clothes so his bottom ended up with carbuncles on it. He became enlightened and a great yogi in his own right . . . all in one lifetime.

Inspiration is related to hope. When we feel inspired, then we feel there is a real possibility of achieving what we want. More than that, inspiration implies that what we are hoping for is something positive. That is for things that help us to develop wisdom and kindness, things which help us to remember our interconnectedness rather than our isolation.

Inspired people not only feel that their life has meaning, but they put that meaning into practice, often against formidable odds. There are inspiring stories to be found in the sports world, in the various arts, in science and politics. The famous boxer Jack Dempsey said, "A champion is one who gets up when he can't."[44] We may be

inspired by any one of these stories. Inspiration is not just a religious
or spiritual phenomenon. Hearing stories of people who have got
through the difficulties we face ourselves gives us the hope that
we can do this too. There are people who have broken through an
addiction like ours. Who are they and how did they do it? Finding
and reading these stories stretches our minds and reminds us that
so much is possible. This is one of the reasons why self-help groups
are so effective. We hear inspiring stories directly related to our own
situation.

But perhaps we feel so down that when we hear these inspiring
stories we feel worse because there seems to be such a huge gap
between where we are at the moment and where this inspirational
person has gotten to. We need to bring our wisdom mind back into
action. We need to remember that they too had to start with small
steps, that they too felt despair before things got better. We need to
remember that it takes time to change old habits and especially the
habit of feeling guilty. We need to bring equanimity back into the
way we see ourselves.

Aspiration refers to the motivations and goals we set for ourselves once we are inspired. When we have achieved what we were
inspired to do, then we look for another inspiration. When one
project is complete, then we look for a new one. In the end, we
face death and that brings up the question of what happens after
death. Can death be inspiring? This is another question to meditate
on. It is a religious and spiritual question. If we want inspiration
to bring us a deep and lasting happiness, then we need to look to
people who have looked at death in the face, the wise people of
this planet. These wise people have lived according to principles or
values which we all recognize as bringing peace and harmony to
us all.

Service: The Doing Part of Loving-Kindness

*"We cannot live for ourselves alone. Our lives are connected by
a thousand invisible threads, and along these sympathetic fibers,
our actions run as causes and return to us as results."*[45]

Service is the doing part of loving-kindness. Love goes with kindness, with wanting to bring peace and joy into someone's life instead of suffering. We can call this quality wisdom-love or compassionate wisdom. The simplest way to love is to do no harm. That is why we need the wisdom side. The best way to love is to have the wisdom to know what will bring deep and lasting happiness—and then to do just that.

If we have been weakened by illness and/or addiction, then the idea of serving others might seem impossible. We need to stop and think about the little acts of service which fit in with what we are able to achieve. At the very least, even if we are very weak, we can send out thoughts and prayers to people who need them. That is an act of service. Smiling at someone, even when we are in pain, can be an act of service. Sometimes we are of service to others even when we do not realize it. If we walk down the street with a happy, relaxed mind, this can be an act of serving the people we simply walk past. There are small acts of kindness and big ones. Being kind means to serve others.

Meditating on service means taking time out to contemplate what we have given to others, no matter how small the gift. It means taking time to contemplate ways in which we might be of service to others, no matter how small.

Courage

Courage is hope in action. It is one thing to have principles, it is another thing to hold to these principles when they are being ridiculed, or when we face the threat of torture for holding them. Courage is an inner strength which arises when we know clearly what we are doing and why we are doing it. Courage arises in the face of opposition.

Opposition is very familiar to people with addictions. There is so much which pushes us back into our addiction trap: people, events, things we see or smell, the various outer and inner triggers that we talked about in the previous chapters. Courage is about continuing to create new habits even when this is difficult.

Courage doesn't mean that we have to get it right the first time. Everyone who is working for positive change in the world has moments when they are tired, anxious, and unsure of themselves. Courage involves a willingness to learn from challenges and difficulties, and to recognize them as learning opportunities. What seem like setbacks may be invaluable opportunities to deepen our understanding and improve our skills. In the process, a sense of humor will be invaluable.

Can you imagine yourself as a courageous person? How would your life be different? What small courageous steps can you take right now? What tools do you need to help you take these steps?

Courage, when it is mixed with endurance and perseverance, is a great benefit to addicted people. It comes from having faith in the possibility of change and determination to carry it through. It is hope in action.

Freedom to Be Happy

We already know that relying on something temporary to bring a lasting happiness is just illogical. What, then, are we going to rely on? For a start, we learn to accept the reality of change. Whatever brings us pleasure, eventually we have to either see it go, or be parted from it. Secondly, we give up the instant gratification trip. Tools for happiness do not include instant gratification. If we look at these sixteen tools for happiness, then we can see that they all consider the needs of others.

How do we give people what they really need? We cannot answer that question without some wisdom. There is no point in being generous with something harmful. So how do we know what will harm and what will not? As we ask those questions we begin to have a deeper understanding of what it means to be a human on this small planet. What enriches life and reconnects us? We cannot reconnect if we are full of pride, arrogance, bitterness, jealousy, depression, or resentment. Wise people often talk about the importance of being connected, of having effective ways to relate to the people we love and respect. As our wisdom develops, we also begin to see that we need to find effective ways of connecting with everything: all people, the whole environment, both material and spiritual.

There is always a danger of becoming discouraged when we compare ourselves with wise people. There seems to be such a big gap. Wise people had to start from somewhere. They did not become wise through some supernatural trickery. Some of this wisdom they may have acquired in previous lifetimes. Such people are born wise. Even for them, there were the hard times to get through. They also experienced suffering and set out to find a way around it.

If we are going to develop wisdom, we have to start from where we are at this moment, not from some theoretically perfect state. We all have different things to learn. We all have wisdom that we have already learned. Even the decision to work through this book is a sign that you have some inner wisdom already there. These lists, like the sixteen guidelines to happiness, give us a clue as to what we are working towards.

As we make an effort to develop wisdom, it helps a lot to have our equanimity tool handy. To create a new habit, we need to repeat it over and over again. We begin by imagining the new way of being as we meditate. How would Duncan do this? Let's say Duncan has decided to practice humility. You can imagine that he would have a lot of trouble. It would be so easy for him to fall back into his old pattern of knowing everything. But he has been reading this book and developing his equanimity tool. This means that when he does fall back into his old patterns, he does not exaggerate and think he is no good. He just notes that he has fallen into it again and takes that as a sign that he needs to continue to develop humility. He decides that since he needs so much practice he is going to make it into a meditation. His meditation is as follows.

First he sets his motivation. He decides that his motivation is to be a more likable person. Then he thinks that maybe that motivation is still too self-seeking. He decides that his motivation will be to learn humility so that he can understand and help others.

He is going to meditate on humility. He first reads as much as he can on the subject so that he has a good idea of what humility is about. He is very keen to understand the difference between humility and being weak. His beginning meditations, then, involve reading and thinking about humility. He finishes each meditation with his dedication: "I have done this meditation so that I can become humble instead of arrogant. In this way, I can help others instead of hurting them."

Once he has the idea of humility clear in his head (and this has taken quite a few weeks), he decides that he can meditate on being humble. He does this, after setting his motivation, by visualizing himself being humble when he is criticized. He tries to imagine lots of different situations in which he might be humble instead of arrogant.

After doing this meditation every day, he begins to catch himself when he is about to be arrogant. He stops himself and practices humility just as he had visualized during his meditation. Sometimes people are pleasantly surprised. Sometimes they do not even notice he has been different. Sometimes they react as if he is not being humble but trying a new and underhanded form of arrogance. Since Duncan has practiced equanimity as well, he is now not caught up in grasping at the perfect response for other people. He accepts their response and does not exaggerate its significance. Of course, this does not happen instantly. Duncan has also learned to be patient and accept that change can take a while

Knowing the wise way to handle any situation does not guarantee that other people will respond the way you want them to. It does not guarantee that you will never fall back into your old patterns. But if you have developed your equanimity tool, these things will no longer be a problem. Instead you will begin to see them as lessons so that you can refine your equanimity tool and whatever of the positive values you are trying to develop in your mind.

The tools that we need to escape from our addiction are the same tools that are used in positive psychology. Positive psychology aims to bring out the best in people. Peter Ralston was the first Westerner to win the world martial arts prize. How did he do this?[46]

One: The starting point: ambition, focused intention.

"As a teenager I wanted to be the best fighter in the world. Period!"

Two: Recognition of the unsatisfactoriness of the ordinary conscious way of doing things (may come with success).

"Around that time, I would go to classes and fight black belts and win, but still feel like I lost . . . Something wasn't right . . . I was winning from natural ability, but I wasn't winning because I really understood anything . . ."

Three: Finding the unbiased mind beyond fear and desire. Opening perceptions. Appreciation.

"It was in that situation that I first learned to drop fear of getting hit, or of winning or losing . . . What that did was open up my perception to what was really happening. I just saw a fist coming and I'd move . . . When I'd get worried about it, I'd get stuck somewhere and get hit . . . It's a beautiful secret, an exacting and tremendous feedback."

Four: Expansion of the knowing field. Also some change in sense of time.

". . . abilities like being able to read somebody's disposition accurately started to come. The moment they would think to hit me I would stop them. That's it. Handled. I just kept finishing everything before it got started."

Five: Actions from awareness; simply knowing what to do and it's always appropriate.

"New abilities started to arise . . . I didn't have to be cognizant of any movement on their part, psychic or otherwise, to know what to do. I just knew. That blew me away. I didn't have to perceive a thing . . . very simple, very simple."

Six: Comes full circle; transformation of the original ambition and intention.

"I decided that if I were to continue to do this, I wanted to start contributing what I did and what I knew in a much larger way. I wanted to transform the martial arts in the world into a place for the development of the human being, and of honesty."

The tools we need to break out of our addictions are the same tools we need to bring out the best in us. In one way, if we are trying to break free from addiction, we are in an incredibly fortunate position because the need to develop these tools is so obvious.

looking ahead:
wisdom, compassion, and happiness

9

Ultimately, humanity is one and this small planet is our only home. If we are to protect this home of ours, each of us needs to experience a vivid sense of universal altruism. It is only this feeling that can remove the self-centered motives that cause people to deceive and misuse one another.

If you have a sincere and open heart, you naturally feel self-worth and confidence, and there is no need to be fearful of others.
—HIS HOLINESS THE DALAI LAMA[47]

THE BIGGEST emotional pain we can suffer is the feeling that life has no meaning. People commit suicide because this pain is so great. They feel they have nothing to contribute, everything they do is pointless. "What is the meaning of life?" is the big philosophical question and there have been many answers to it.

Life suddenly has meaning when there is something urgent to be done such as when we fall in love or when we create an interesting project. But when the love affair or project is over, then what? We have nothing meaningful to do. We become depressed.

"Falling in love" is what we say when we become attracted to a potential partner. Falling in love, or romantic love, usually means "I want this person to make me complete because I am inadequate by myself." This is what Cindy in Chapter 3 did. She was not really so concerned about her potential husband, but about herself. Suddenly she had a great hope that her dream for herself would be complete. Everything she did for her future husband was to make him like her and he would then complete her dream. Each time her dream falls apart she reaches for her alcohol. Most of us have done the same thing at some stage in our lives. Then when the manipulation does not work, we become angry with the person who was supposed to make our dream come true, and maybe depressed about ourselves.

When we mix love with wisdom, we want our friends to be happy. Wisdom-love means that for a time we are focused on what that person needs, not on ourselves. Wisdom-love even recognizes that our enemies want to be happy. His Holiness the Dalai Lama does not hate the Chinese, who have overrun Tibet. Instead he sees that the Chinese who have tortured his people and invaded his nation are suffering deeply from ignorance, greed, and fear. Wisdom-love helped Nelson Mandela introduce the idea of forgiveness towards the same people who imprisoned him and killed many black South Africans.

People like the Dalai Lama and Nelson Mandela inspire us because they live with wisdom-love. They don't just talk about it. They show us that wisdom-love is a real possibility and that it has the potential to reunite, to reconnect people. Wisdom-love is the inspiration behind heartfelt forgiveness. Since addiction makes us disconnected, then developing wisdom-love can heal that rift. If we cannot develop wisdom-love towards the people who have harmed us, then perhaps we can learn its skills by using wisdom-love as a volunteer, or caring for an animal, or by being generous, or whatever else works for you

When we have meaning in our lives, we are inspired. To be inspired means, literally, to take a deep breath in. We become inseparable from air, from the environment.

How to Develop Wisdom-Love: Introducing Bodhichitta

Cindy thought she was in love, but we can see that this was a pseudolove which lacked wisdom. As she learns more about the way she tends to manipulate others, she will begin to see that genuine love is based on wanting the best for the other person. Genuine and wise love is the opposite of the actions of addictive patterns. It is more concerned with the needs of the other person than with ourselves. This does not mean that we do not look after ourselves, but that we see our own needs in the context of the needs of others, and choose what is important on that basis.

Buddhism teaches us that these "others" are not just our family and friends but also our enemies, all the creatures on this planet, including the rats and cockroaches and funnel web spiders. The wisdom behind this is the recognition that even the rats, cockroaches, and spiders simply want to be happy. Then Buddhism goes one step further and says that there is a complex web of interaction, including the nasties, that brings us to where we are now and the benefits we have in this lifetime. This is taught by saying that all beings have been our mothers in some past lifetime simply because we have had countless previous lifetimes and so have had countless rebirths in different forms. We owe them all something.

It is not so easy to work out what a funnel web spider needs for its happiness. We would need a much deeper wisdom about spiders to know that. Even with our friends it is difficult to know what will bring them happiness. Our friends might ask for money for their gambling addiction and would be pleased if we gave it to them, but this would not bring them deeper happiness. Again, we need wisdom to know how to benefit Duncan and his gambling.

Being kind by itself is not enough. If kindness by itself is to be helpful, then it needs a good dose of wisdom added to it. *Bodhichitta* is a Buddhist term that refers to this coming together of wisdom and kindness in its most extensive form—the mind that understands reality as it is without any delusions. Buddhists call this the wisdom realizing emptiness, meaning that reality is empty of any deluded way of thinking about it. The most extensive form of kindness is that which wants to remove all suffering and bring happiness to any sentient being (a being with a mind) without exception.

When Buddhists set their motivation for a meditation, they include this extensive twofold bodhichitta motivation: "May I realize emptiness so that I can be of unwavering benefit to all sentient beings without exception." If you are not a Buddhist, then you can reword this bodhichitta motivation to fit your own religion or life philosophy: "May I fully complete my spiritual path, attain an omniscient mind, so that I always know how to be of benefit to any sentient being that comes into contact with me."

The meditations on wise loving-kindness help us with this bodhichitta motivation. We practice a mind of equanimity to friends, enemies, and strangers. To do that, we also develop further the tool of equanimity towards different aspects of our own minds: our potential, our limitations, and everything else.

Meditation 12: Wise Loving-Kindness

Once again we relax our body and focus on our breathing. We allow the breathing to naturally become quiet, not forcing it in any way. As our breathing calms down, our mind also calms down. This happens of its own accord. If your mind wanders, then gently bring it back to the focus of meditation, the simple awareness of the breath going in and out. Stay on this for a moment.

From within this calmness and clarity, think about how good it feels to experience wise and loving kindness from someone. Think about the warmth in your heart when you generate loving-kindness and wisdom towards the people you love.

The essence of mind is pure, without any distortion. The mind has incredible potential for compassionate wisdom.

Motivation

Return to the calmness and clarity for a while. From within that space develop your personal motivation for doing the meditation. Then include your personal motivation in this extensive motivation: "I would like to give to other people the same unwavering pure compassionate wisdom that I would like given to me. To do that, I need to develop my own compassionate wisdom and, if I am to develop my own compassionate wisdom, then I need to be constantly in touch with completely pure compassionate wisdom. For this reason I will now tune in to the pure compassionate wisdom energy and then meditate on wise loving-kindness."

Tuning in to pure compassionate wisdom

We can imagine this pure compassionate wisdom in the form of white light which surrounds us all the time. We can choose to allow this light into our body and mind so that it can remove all the dark pain, all the dark negative thoughts and feelings. Allowing ourselves to be bathed in this white healing light of compassionate wisdom can be a meditation in itself.

Wise loving-kindness towards oneself

Even though our minds can become completely pure and wise, so often we find ourselves feeling angry and hurt, grasping and arrogant. These mental disturbances cause so much suffering in our minds. Knowing this, we generate the desire to be free of these mental disturbances and the suffering they create.

So recognizing our shortcomings, and also our potential, we generate strongly the wish, the prayer, to be free:

May I be free of sorrow, hurt, anger, greed, arrogance, jealousy, and all such mental afflictions.

May I be free from the suffering that arises from such afflictions.

May I recognize and cultivate loving-kindness and compassion, patience and generosity, and all other good qualities.

May I experience the sense of well-being, of joy and bliss, of calmness and clarity which arise when I am happy.

May I develop profound quietness of mind that allows me to develop great insight and deep compassion.

In this way, may I be well and happy.

May I be a source of similar peace and joy and well-being to all those people whom I love and, indeed, all people and creatures with whom I have contact, and even those people and creatures I have never met.

Imagine these things to be so now, as realistically as you can. Imagine it to be so right now.

We stay with that thought for a while.

Wise loving-kindness towards someone I love

Now we bring to mind some **person we love dearly**, feeling the warmth and openness in your heart as you bring this person to mind.

Think: "This person, like me, is endowed with the pure clarity and incredible potential of mind. Yet, like me, this person also gets entangled in negative emotions and experiences mental suffering. This person, like me, also wishes to be free of suffering and to experience only joy and peace and wisdom and clarity."

With this in mind, think:

May this person, like myself, be free of sorrow, hurt, anger, greed, arrogance, jealousy, and all such mental afflictions.

May this person be free from the suffering that arises from such afflictions.

May this person recognize and cultivate loving-kindness and compassion, patience and generosity, and all other good qualities.

May this person experience the sense of well-being, of joy and bliss, of calmness and clarity which arise as the positive qualities flourish.

May this person develop the profound quietness of mind that allows him or her to develop great insight and deep compassion.

In this way, may this person be well and happy.

May this person, and all people he or she loves, be a source of similar peace and joy and well-being to all those people whom they also love and, indeed, all people and creatures with whom they also have contact, and even those people and creatures they have never met.

Imagine these things to be so for this person you love now, as realistically as you can. Feel the warmth in your heart as you send these positive qualities to that person.

We stay with that thought for a while.

Wise loving-kindness towards people I neither love nor hate

Now we bring to mind some **person who triggers neither love nor hate**. This could be someone who passes us on the street, or who sells us the newspaper, or who sits opposite us on the train. We try to generate the same strength of the warmth and openness in our heart to this person as we did for the person we love.

Think: "This person, like me, is endowed with the pure clarity and incredible potential of mind. Yet, like me, this person also gets entangled in negative emotions and experiences mental suffering. This person, like me, also wishes to be free of suffering and to experience only joy and peace and wisdom and clarity."

With this in mind, think:

May this person, like myself, be free of sorrow, hurt, anger, greed, arrogance, jealousy, and all such mental afflictions.

May this person be free from the suffering that arises from such afflictions.

May this person recognize and cultivate loving-kindness and compassion, patience and generosity, and all other good qualities.

May this person experience the sense of well-being, of joy and bliss, of calmness and clarity which arise as the positive qualities flourish.

May this person develop the profound quietness of mind that allows him or her to develop great insight and deep compassion.

In this way, may this person be well and happy.

May this person, and all people he or she loves, be a source of similar peace and joy and well-being to all those people whom they also love and, indeed, all people and creatures with whom they also have contact, and even those people and creatures they have never met.

Imagine these things to be so for this person you love now, as realistically as you can. Feel the warmth in your heart as you send these positive qualities to that person.

We stay with that thought for a while.

Wise loving-kindness towards people I fear or hate

Finally, we visualize **a person whom we actively dislike, or hate, or fear** and bring this person strongly to our mind.

Think: "Whatever it is about this person that makes him or her so objectionable to me, these are the same qualities that I experience in my own mind that create my own suffering. Try to generate the same strength of loving-kindness towards this person as you did towards the person you love.

"This person, like me, is endowed with the pure clarity and incredible potential of mind. Yet, like me, this person also gets entangled in negative emotions and experiences mental suffering. This person, like myself, also wishes to be free of suffering and to experience only joy and peace and wisdom and clarity. If he or she could be free of suffering, then there would be no reason for me to fear or hate him or her."

With these thoughts in mind, think strongly:

May this person, like myself, be free of sorrow, hurt, anger, greed, arrogance, jealousy, and all such mental afflictions.

May this person be free from the suffering that arises from such afflictions.

May this person recognize and cultivate loving-kindness and compassion, patience and generosity, and all other good qualities.

May this person experience the sense of well-being, of joy and bliss, of calmness and clarity which arise as the positive qualities flourish.

May this person develop the profound quietness of mind that allows him or her to develop great insight and deep compassion.

In this way, may this person be well and happy.

May this person, and all people he or she loves, be a source of similar peace and joy and well-being to all those people whom they also love and, indeed, all people and creatures with whom they also have contact, and even those people and creatures they have never met.

Imagine these things to be so for this person you love now, as realistically as you can. Feel the warmth in your heart as you send these positive qualities to that person.

We stay with that thought for a while.

Closing the meditation

In this way, unlimited loving kindness and compassion arise in our hearts in the nature of radiant white light which is the very essence of one's own true nature. This white light arises from the inexhaustible source of ultimate wisdom and great compassion and suffuses every cell of your body, cleansing it of all impurities, mental and physical.

Your ordinary body becomes completely pure and the light within can no longer be contained, but radiates in all four directions of the compass, and up and down. This inexhaustible light fills those people you love, those you hate, and those you do not particularly care about. They all receive the same radiant loving-kindness, the same wishes for their happiness, for their freedom from all suffering. The rays of light illuminate all places. Where there is poverty, it brings wealth. Where there is famine, it brings food. Where there is disease, it brings health. Where there is fear, it brings peace of mind, courage, and joy. In this way, the whole earth, and even beyond the earth, is transformed into the same radiant white light.

And now the white light returns to us. Our bodies become bodies of light and our minds rest in peace and clarity.

We stay in this peace and clarity as long as we can.

Dedication

We finish the meditation by dedicating the power of this practice to our individual well-being, and also to the well-being of all creatures without exception, to the peace of the entire world so that each one from the tiniest to the most powerful and including ourselves can really attain that purity of mind and infinite love and wisdom that we have imagined.

Putting It All Together

Without understanding how your inner nature evolves, how can you possibly discover eternal happiness? Where is eternal happiness? It's not in the sky or in the jungle; you won't find it in the air or under the ground. Everlasting happiness is within you, within your psyche, your consciousness, your mind. That's why it's important that you investigate the nature of your own mind.
—LAMA YESHE[48]

Learning how to escape from addiction is really no different than learning how to deal with other problems in our lives. There always seems to be something more, something better just around the corner. We will find a simple cure for our health problems, or we will soon have plenty of money, or the ideal job or partner, or a car is just about to appear. For most of us, life is a continual round of temporary satisfactions inevitably disrupted by some dissatisfaction or other.

Having explored this book, contemplated and meditated on different tools for cutting addictive patterns, it is time to review what we know about the sources of our happiness. Our sources of inspiration in our search for happiness are those people who have found peace and joy in their everyday lives, regardless of their income level or health or living conditions or notoriety. It is also time to believe in ourselves: to take with both hands the possibility of change ... lovingly ... as if that possibility is a baby to be nurtured. It is time to put into practice any compassionate wisdom we may have acquired.

We may not be able to choose what this world throws at us, but we can choose the way in which we react to those things, both the good and the bad. If we react through exaggerating, we make it all the more difficult. If we can learn to react with equanimity, being able to see clearly, then we are in a better position to deal with whatever comes. When we learn not to overreact, we find we are better able to know the pain of people around us, even if we cannot help them. We find that we connect, too, with their joy.

If we work towards this connectedness, then we find a quality of happiness that is not found in the high or numbness of addictive patterns. We discover a way of eliminating the pain of being unloved, unwanted, unrecognized. This interconnectedness is the invisible threads that bind us all. As we become more and more aware of our connections, we find them creeping out from our heart and including all people and creatures, whether we like them or not. We have begun to see the suffering and delight this planet has for us. We begin to feel that pure compassionate wisdom is something we can recognize and touch and be touched by. The sense of unfulfilled spiritual yearning drops away.

All this might sound magical if it were not for the fact that there have been rare people, stretching back to the dim depths of history, who have said that this has been their experience. "Love one another as I have loved you," said Jesus Christ. His Holiness the Dalai Lama says that spirituality is a human journey into our internal resources, with the aim of understanding who we are in the deepest sense—and of discovering how to live according to the highest possible ideal.[49]

Wisdom

Wisdom has to do with seeing things as they are, which helps us find effective ways of understanding how they connect. Just as the Buddha sat under the Bodhi tree and examined his mind until he attained enlightenment, we also need to examine our minds if we want to become wise.

If we want to see what our minds are like and to measure any change, then we have to do it ourselves, through looking inwards, applying introspection. We can sometimes measure the effectiveness of changes we have made by seeing how other people relate to us. But as Carri found out in most versions of her story, this is not always a good indicator. If we are going to check our minds through looking inwards, then we also need to do this with the same honesty and objectivity that a scientist uses to check external things.

When we look at our minds with an honest and objective wisdom, then we find that our thoughts and feelings and emotions are always changing. We can also find that we can consciously choose and train our minds to think about one thing and not another. This means we have some control. We can develop that control through meditation and through real-life practice. As we do that, we develop a soundly based confidence.

Wisdom also tells us that the things and people out there that we rely on to bring us pleasure are also impermanent. They pass away or we pass away. New connections develop, stay a while, then also pass away. The only thing we can rely on to bring us happiness is the equanimity in our own minds which recognizes this truth and is not upset by it.

If we are going to rely on our minds, then we also need to know when we are being fooled by our own thoughts. Underneath all our mistaken beliefs is the belief that we are somehow fixed and unchangeable. This idea has been with us since we could first speak and even before then. It is the idea that when I use the word "I" to refer to myself, that this is forever unchanging, forever independent of any other thought, forever independent of my age, my education, and specially independent from my parents. The Buddha taught that this is simply untrue. Not only is it a misguided view, but it lies underneath all the suffering we cause to ourselves and to others. Wisdom sees through this false view and replaces it with the view that nothing exists without being dependent on something else. We exist in a web of interdependence which we can influence for better or worse. Buddhists call this web "dependent-arising." The possibility of change is always present because we exist within this web of dependent-arising. When we understand what dependent-arising means, we realize we are all connected with each other, whether we are aware of this or not.

Wise Compassion

When we find ourselves getting caught in negative emotions, if we check carefully, we will come to see that something has threatened "me" or "mine." There has been a threat to our carefully constructed ego.

Every negative thought or habit comes from trying to protect this self-serving ego. Anything that seems to protect this ego we hang on to, even when logically we know it is damaging. If anything threatens the ego, we have a strong aversion to it. We get rid of it as quickly as we can. The grim hanging on to and exaggerating what we think is good and aversion to what we think is bad give rise to all the other negative emotions. Every time we experience a negative feeling we have the opportunity to do some research into our ego and expose it for what it is.

We have also seen that breaking the hold of addiction, including addiction to our carefully constructed ego, needs to be balanced by building positive qualities and values as tools for our future. Those positive qualities are the ones which develop a wise connection between us and others. This means that every time we take the needs and happiness of others as our main perspective, we are loosening the hold of addiction. Every time we act with compassion and loving-kindness, we are undermining our addiction.

Breaking the addiction trap is to break into a new understanding of oneself which is grounded on the kindness of countless people and animals, which recognizes one's own pain and the pain of others, and which is connected to pure compassionate wisdom that shines on us all, wise or not. Breaking the addiction trap is to be rich in our possibility for happiness.

The wisdom we get through saying "Enough!" and making an effort to break the addiction trap becomes the wisdom that can be developed to give us deeper and deeper understanding about the meaning of life. When we look at the lives of wise people and think about how they became wise, then we have a chance of becoming wise ourselves. Very often we find that such people have a deep spiritual awareness.

Lasting Happiness

What is lasting happiness? It cannot be anything subject to change, otherwise it would not be lasting. It is not something which takes us out of this world in which we live, otherwise it would be partial. It has words to describe it like "contentment," "peace," "openness," "being at home with ourselves and the world." It experiences pleasure in its fullness and also pain in its fullness, but without any ignorance or exaggeration or grasping or aversion.

It seems as if such happiness is unattainable, but Buddhism says we can definitely get there. The spiritual path of any valid religion gives us the training to reach that point. Meanwhile, we swing between two views. On the one hand, we look at the end result, remembering the wise people who are further ahead on the path. On the other hand, we look at ourselves and where we are on that path, but we look at ourselves in a particular way. Instead of our old ways of seeing ourselves through the dark glasses of ignorance, exaggerations, aversions, and clinging, we see ourselves with tools such as equanimity and patience. We see ourselves as part of the huge web of humanity. We see ourselves as being able to choose to tune in to pure compassionate wisdom instead of foolishness and greed. We know our strengths and our limitations, so we can think and act and relate to others with a soundly based self-confidence. Our life has meaning.

I hope that you understand what the word "spiritual" really means. It means to search for, to investigate, the true nature of the mind. There's nothing spiritual outside. My rosary isn't spiritual; my robes aren't spiritual. Spiritual means the mind, and spiritual people are those who seek its nature. —LAMA YESHE[50]

appendix 1:
explanation for professionals

IN BRINGING this book together, I have been informed by aca-
demic research into effective methods for working with addicted
people. Many of these methods combine cognitive therapies with
Buddhist teachings. While I will not present a literature review here,
this has been done elsewhere and references are cited below. The
meditations and suggestions in this book can be used as a self-help
medium or in conjunction with either personal therapies or group
work. While much of the research on the effectiveness of meditation in preventing relapse from addiction is related to Vipassana
meditation, the meditations in this book involve mindfulness and
visualizations as used in Tibetan Buddhism. These meditations are
comparable to the cue-exposure techniques of cognitive behavioral
therapy (CBT) and involve cognitive restructuring to facilitate better coping strategies and improved relationships.

Theories of addiction are many and varied. West (2001) summarizes them in five groups: (1) theories that attempt to provide
broad insight into the conceptualization of addiction, (2) theories
that try to explain why some stimuli are more potent in triggering
addiction, (3) theories about why some people are more susceptible
to addictions, (4) the environmental and social conditions precipi-
tating addiction, and (5) theories about recovery and relapse. Like
most theories, the actuality is that all these approaches are needed to
cut the root of an addiction. Marlatt and Witkiewitz (2005) list the
following determinants of lapse and relapse: self-efficacy, outcome
expectancies, motivation, coping skills, emotional states, craving,
and social support. All of these are addressed in way or another in
this book.

Many of the Buddhist teachings are psychological in their application and use similar determinants. For example, teachings on thought transformation (e.g., Zopa 1994) and the eightfold noble path[51] have the same rationale and therefore the same validation as CBT; that is, thoughts interact with feelings and actions. Buddhism, like other religions, recognizes that thought grounded in wisdom will have a positive effect on behavior. CBT has been widely used in addiction treatment (e.g., Cilente 2001 and Marlatt and Witkiewitz 2005). It has been greatly improved through the addition of mindfulness practices adopted from Buddhist teachings by Kabat-Zinn (2003) and others for a variety of psychosomatic ailments,[52] where it is known as MBCT (Mindfulness-Based Cognitive Therapy).

Other Buddhist practices have been applied to addiction by professionals, academics, and recovered addicts in various ways (Dudley-Grant 2003 and Marlatt and Gordon 1985). These adaptations include using the eightfold noble path, the teachings on mindfulness (Marlatt 2002), or rewriting the twelve steps of Alcoholics Anonymous for Buddhist practitioners (Littlejohn 2009).

I have chosen to use the approach from Buddhism which emphasizes the problems of cravings that arise from attachment, which in Buddhism means "craving."[53] Neurological studies of craving (e.g., Anton 1999 and McCusker 2001) demonstrate a neuroanatomic basis for craving which needs to be given due recognition since it sheds insight into habit formation and degeneration of habits. "Incorporating the methods of imaginal or *in vivo* cue-exposure, while attending to and exploring the cognitive elements of the experience, may facilitate [awareness of implicit positive propositions] given the situational and cue-dependent nature of memory processes." (McCusker 2001, 54). While neuroanatomy is beyond the purpose of this book, learning how to undo an ingrained habit is not. The meditations can be understood as forms of imaginal cue-exposure in which, as Marlatt (1994, 180) puts it, "the client is taught to be mindfully aware of the conditioned response to the cue (craving and/or the urge to indulge)."

Attachment, in the Buddhist sense, refers to the mind that overrates the positive aspects of a person or thing and grasps at the unrealistic dream that follows. It is not hard to see that this use of "attachment" is related to what we mean by addiction and applies to cognitive models of addiction. In Buddhism, one of the principal methods for overcoming attachment is the application of equanimity (or "nonjudgmentalism," to use the terminology of MBCT). I have avoided "nonjudgmentalism" as a term since, although one is not being judgmental in terms of the material arising during mindfulness practice, there is nevertheless the intention to replace irrational and ineffective thoughts with rational and effective thoughts. One therefore makes a judgment about what is effective. Equanimity more closely applies to that feature of not being thrown around emotionally by one's cravings, attachments, and aversions.

Equanimity implies certain values, which is why values and wisdom form a significant component of this book. CBT now also recognizes the importance of values. Value-centered intervention arose from questioning the target of therapy (Wilson and Murrell 2003) and specifically in contrast to the "pleasant events" approach of earlier CBT practice. If the "wellness" target of psychotherapy is to enable a full and meaningful life, then it must include wisdom and compassion. This is the approach of Mindfulness-integrated Cognitive Behavior Therapy (Cayoun and Elbourne 2008).

The more difficult task is to describe a rationale for a spiritual dimension in effectively breaking addictive patterns. While this has been a key part of Alcoholics Anonymous and is obviously a component in religious organizations devoted to addiction, its transcendental and mystical aspects have not been clearly separated from religious dogma.

While many people have a sense of spirituality, they often find that religions do not meet their need for spiritual growth. It is not enough for professionals to ignore this dimension or to send their clients/patients to a religious leader. Nor is it enough to dismiss people with a spiritual awareness as New Age nuts. Rather, the overlap between psychological healing and spiritual healing needs to be both acknowledged and specified. Batchelor (2007) and Bien and Bien (2002) have produced books giving practical guidelines and including the spiritual dimension.

Spirituality in this book refers firstly to a yearning towards completeness. Spiritual completeness is defined according to Buddhist teachings as pure wisdom and compassion. Similarly, in Christianity, God is both omniscient and loving. On the basis of Buddhist teachings, I have accepted that such completeness is achievable and that there are ways to do this. A second way of viewing spirituality is in terms of connection with the fully purified mind, in other words, prayer. We know that we are likely to adopt the values and behavior of the company we keep. This is why keeping in touch with compassionate wisdom is so important. At the simplest level, this means keeping company with people who are wise and compassionate, whether physically or in terms of their writing. This book, therefore, focuses on the aspects of spirituality as recognition of and tuning in to wisdom and compassion rather than emphasizing subtle or mystical states of consciousness. This allows for a more grounded approach to spirituality which is compatible with the major religions as well as those who profess a spiritual awareness independent of religious institutions.

All Buddhist traditions have key texts which have been translated into English and there are many books in a more user-friendly format. Of these, perhaps the most useful coming from my own tradition is Yangsi (2003), who gives an eminently readable description of the Lam Rim (the Graduated Path to Enlightenment), which has been the source of so much of my Buddhist understanding. This path was initially developed by Lama Atisha specifically for the Tibetans and later extensively explained by Lama Tsong Khapa. Hopkins (1983) provides a deeper discussion of many aspects of Buddhist psychology based on the Abhidharma[54] which do not appear in the Lam Rim but which are part of monastic training.

appendix 2:
the twelve steps of alcoholics anonymous

- We admitted we were powerless over alcohol—that our lives had become unmanageable.
- Came to believe that a Power greater than ourselves could restore us to sanity.
- Made a decision to turn our will and our lives over to the care of God *as we understood Him*.
- Made a searching and fearless moral inventory of ourselves.
- Admitted to God, to ourselves, and to another human being the exact nature of our wrongs.
- Were entirely ready to have God remove all these defects of character.
- Humbly asked Him to remove our shortcomings.
- Made a list of all persons we had harmed, and became willing to make amends to them all.
- Made direct amends to such people wherever possible, except when to do so would injure them or others.
- Continued to take personal inventory and when we were wrong promptly admitted it.
- Sought through prayer and meditation to improve our conscious contact with God, *as we understood Him*, praying only for knowledge of His will for us and the power to carry that out.
- Having had a spiritual awakening as the result of these Steps, we tried to carry this message to alcoholics, and to practice these principles in all our affairs.

appendix 3:
the buddhist eightfold noble path as described in workshops on addiction[55]

Right Understanding

- Impermanence is a fact of life; therefore, addiction can be and is impermanent. The satisfaction derived from addiction is also impermanent. Change is always possible.
- Everything changes, even addiction. Using the substance may give short-term benefits but does not solve the underlying problem, which needs to be understood.
- Reflection on impermanence is part of right understanding.
- Accepting addiction and shining the light on the pain is also included in right understanding.

Right Thought

- Being reflective of our perceptions enables us to break self-cherishing thoughts: by thinking of others we aren't thinking of ourselves, and therefore we won't be tempted or need to satisfy our addiction.
- What we think creates our reality—change your thought, change your life! We can choose positive thinking patterns to overcome craving. By overcoming our self-cherishing we will overcome our addiction.
- Choose positive thoughts.

Right Speech

- Speak to others as you would like them to speak to you.
- If we hurt ourselves or others with our speech, this is a trigger for our addiction.
- Practice truthful, helpful, thoughtful words.

Right Action

- There are alternative actions to going into addictions.
- Right action means putting into practice what we have developed; for example, practicing giving to others.

Right Livelihood

- Be kind to everything and everyone in the world. Everyone is treated equally.
- If our work harms others, it harms us either now or in the future—and then we use the substance to numb that pain.
- Show consideration and love for all living beings.
- Practice generosity.

Right Effort

- Right effort includes a constant awareness of others. We can make an effort to be sensitive to the struggles of other people with addictions because we know what it is like. We can make an effort to be aware of how our addictions have affected others.
- It includes creating the right environment, e.g., not associating with old "using" friends.
- It helps us break negative habitual patterns and create new positive patterns.

Right Mindfulness

- No pain, no gain.
- Right mindfulness is helped by meditation.
- Without mindfulness, the other aspects of the path are not possible.
- Thought comes before action and speech.

Right Meditation or Concentration

- Concentration is about prioritizing what's important in our lives.
- It is developed through meditation.
- Concentration focuses the mind, giving clarity concerning problems.
- Through concentration and meditation we unlock the addiction trap.

appendix 4
some useful websites

http://www.spiritualriver.com/Addiction_Help_Guide.pdf

http://the12stepbuddhist.com/addiction%20and%20Buddhism/
addiction-and-buddhism

http://www.buddhistrecovery.org/links.htm

http://www.experiencefestival.com/addiction_and_spirituality

http://www.readingaddiction.com/

notes

1 Yeshe (2003), 64-65.
2 Rickwood et al. (2005), 34.
3 The twelve steps of Alcoholics Anonymous are found in Appendix 2.
4 *Dhammapada*, verse 80, trans. Thanissaro Bhikkhu; http://www.accesstoinsight.org/tipitaka/kn/dhp/dhp.06.than.html
5 Corinthians 13:13
6 See (U.S.) President's Council on Bioethics, Staff Working Paper (2003): http://www.bioethics.gov/background/better_memories.html
7 Yeshe (2003), 68.
8 See, for example, Doidge (2007) or Siegel (2007).
9 See Cayoun and Elbourne (2008).
10 See http://www.freedomfromed.com/main/page_recovery_stories.html
11 Of course, use your own label here.
12 Yeshe (2008), 3.
13 Marlatt and Gordon (1985).
14 Yeshe (2000), 126.
15 Cayoun (2008).
16 See, for example, Doidge (2007).
17 Yeshe (2003), 105-6.
18 Yeshe (2003), 8.
19 Yeshe (2003), 43.
20 Yeshe (2008), 51-52.
21 (U.S.) President's Council on Bioethics, Staff Working Paper (2003). See http://www.bioethics.gov/background/better_memories.html
22 Dowrick (1997), 33.
23 The incidence of mental health problems is higher amongst addicts than in the general population. See, e.g., Rickwood et al. (2005), 13-14.
24 This meditation is adapted from meditations introduced to the Healing Group at Tara Institute in Melbourne by Bob Sharples. See Sharples (2006).
25 Anh-Huong was a refugee from Vietnam in 1979 and is now a Buddhist teacher and author. She lives in Northern Virginia and teaches meditation with her husband. She is the niece of Buddhist teacher Thich Nhat Hanh. Quote from Anh-Huong (n.d.), 2.
26 Keenan (1992), 285.

27 A. Einstein et al. (1931), 3.
28 From a speech in the British Parliament on Sept. 9, 1941.
29 Zopa (1994), 56-58.
30 Joseph Michael Straczynski is an award-winning American writer/producer of television series, novels, short stories, comic books, and radio dramas. The quote is from the internet site "Lurker's Guide to Babylon 5: 'Passing Through Gethsemane': jms speaks" (13 July 2004).
31 Matthew 25:13
32 Helen Keller was both blind and deaf after a childhood illness. Quote from Keller (1933).
33 Steinbeck (1954), 20.
34 Tolstoi (1902), 281. In the original quote, "meaning of life" is translated as "vocation."
35 Zopa (1994), 111.
36 Aeschylus (525 BC-456 BC) was a playwright of ancient Greece. The quote is from *Agamemnon*. See http://en.wikiquote.org/wiki/Aeschylus.
37 Yangsi (2003), 480-81.
38 The ten nonvirtues are: killing, stealing, sexual misconduct, lying, divisive speech, harsh talk, idle talk, craving/coveting, ill will, and wrong view.
39 John 15:13
40 The Noble Eightfold Path includes 1) Right Understanding, 2) Right Thought, 3) Right Speech, 4) Right Action, 5) Right Livelihood, 6) Right Effort, 7) Right Mindfulness, and 8) Right Meditation or Concentration. See Appendix 3 for a version derived from workshops on addiction.
41 www.freewebs.com/16guidelines
42 Shah (1972), 133.
43 http://thinkexis t.com/quotes/jean_claude_killy/
44 http://www.quotationsforinspiration.com/gen.htm
45 Frequently attributed to Herman Melville, but written by an evangelical preacher, Henry Melvill. See http://en.wikiquote.org/wiki/Melville
46 See Rosch (2002).
47 From "Compassion and the Individual": http://www.dalailama.com/page.166.htm
48 Yeshe (2003), 42.
49 Dalai Lama (2005), 220.
50 Yeshe (2003), 108.
51 See Bankart, Dockett, and Dudley-Grant (2002).
52 Meta-reviews of mindfulness theory and research have been undertaken by Germer (2005) and Baer (2003), amongst others.
53 Attachment here is not to be confused with the psychoanalytic meaning of the term but is defined as an overvaluing of the positive qualities of an object and is therefore consistent with the psychological components of craving.
54 Early Buddhism analyzed experience into five *skandhas*, or aggregates, and also eighteen *dhatus*, or elements. Later schools developed the Abhidharma; these treatises were collected in the *Abhidharmapitaka,* one of the three main divisions of the Pali Buddhist canon.
55 This list contains lightly edited descriptions created by workshop groups.

bibliography

There are many books which can be used to follow up the ideas presented in this book. Those with an asterisk are recommended for general reading.

Anh-Huong. (n.d.). "Forgiveness and Buddhism." Retrieved June 2009 from http://www.thepowerofforgiveness.com/pdf/Forgiveness_in_Buddhism. pdf.

Anton, R.F. (1999). "What Is Craving? Models and Implications for Treatment." *Alcohol Research and Health* 23 (3): 165-73. Retrieved May 2009 from http://dionysus.psych.wisc.edu/Lit/Articles/AntonR1999a.pdf.

Baer, R. A. (2003). "Mindfulness Training as a Clinical Intervention: A Conceptual and Empirical Review." *Clinical Psychology: Science and Practice* 10:125-43.

Bankart, C.P., K.H. Dockett, and G.R. Dudley-Grant (2002). "On the Path of the Buddha: A Psychologist's Guide to the History of Buddhism." In K.H. Dockett, G.R. Dudley-Grant, and C.P. Bankart, eds., *Psychology and Buddhism: From Individual to Global Community.* New York: Kluwer Academic/ Plenum Publishers.

★ Batchelor, M. (2007). *Let Go: A Buddhist Guide to Breaking Free of Habits.* Boston: Wisdom Publications.

★ Bien, T., and B. Bien. (2002). *Mindful Recovery: A Spiritual Path to Healing from Addiction.* New York: John Wiley.

Cayoun, Bruno. (2008). *MiCBT: Mindfulness-integrated Cognitive Therapies: General Principles and Guidelines.* Tasmania: Uniprint, University of Tasmania.

Cayoun, B., and K. Elbourne. (2008). "What is MiCBT?" Retrieved May 2009 from http://www.mindfulness.net.au/pdf/Intro%20to%20MiCBT.PDF.

Cilente, J. (2001). "Cognitive Theory in Substance Abuse." Retrieved November 2006 from http://www.mental-health-matters/com/articles.

Dalai Lama. (2005). *The Universe in a Single Atom.* New York: Morgan Road Books.

★ Doidge, N. (2007). *The Brain That Changes Itself.* Melbourne: Scribe.

★ Dowrick, Stephanie. (1997). *Forgiveness and Other Acts of Love.* Camberwell, Australia: Penguin Books.

Dudley-Grant, G. Rita. (2003). "Buddhism, Psychology and Addiction Theory in Psychotherapy." In K.H. Docket, G.R. Dudley-Grant, and C.P. Bankart, eds., *Psychology and Buddhism: From Individual to Global Community.* New York: Kluwer Academic/ Plenum Publishers.

Einstein, A., et al. (1931). *Living Philosophies.* New York: Simon and Schuster.

Germer, C. K. (2005). "Mindfulness. What Is It and Does It Matter?" In C. K. Germer, R.D. Siegel, and P. Fulton, eds., *Mindfulness and Psychotherapy.* New York: Guilford Press.

Hopkins, Jeffrey. (1983). *Meditation on Emptiness.* Boston: Wisdom Publications.

Kabat-Zinn, J. (2003). "Mindfulness-Based Interventions in Context: Past, Present, and Future." *Clinical Psychology: Science and Practice* 10 (2): 144–56.

Keenan, Brian. (1992). *An Evil Cradling.* London: Hutchinson.

Keller, H. (1933). "The Simplest Way to Be Happy." *Home Magazine* (February, 1933). See http://www.afb.org/section.asp?SectionID=1&TopicID=193&SubTopicID=12&DocumentID=1211

★Littlejohn, Darren. (2009). *The 12-Step Buddhist: Enhance Recovery from Any Addiction.* Hillsboro, OR: Beyond Words.

McCusker, C.G. (2001). "Cognitive Biases and Addiction: An Evolution in Theory and Methods." *Addiction* 96:47–56.

Marlatt, G.A. (1994). "Addiction, Mindfulness, and Acceptance." In S.C. Hayes, N.S. Jacobson, V.M. Follette, and M.J. Dougher, eds., *Acceptance and Change: Content and Context in Psychotherapy.* Reno, NV: Context Press.

Marlatt, G.A. (2002). "Buddhist Philosophy and the Treatment of Addictive Behaviour." *Cognitive and Behavioral Practice* 9:42–50.

Marlatt, G.A., and J.R. Gordon. (1985). *Relapse Prevention: Maintenance Strategies in the Treatment of Addictive Behaviors.* New York: Guilford Press.

Marlatt, G.A., and K. Witkiewitz. (2005). "Relapse Prevention for Alcohol and Drug Problems." In G.A. Marlatt and D.M. Donovon, eds., *Relapse Prevention: Maintenance Strategies in the Treatment of Addictive Behaviours.* 2nd ed. New York: Guilford Press.

Rickwood, D., et al. (2005). *Perspectives in Psychology: Drug Abuse.* Melbourne: The Australian Psychological Society.

Rosch, Eleanor. (2002). "What Buddhist Meditation has to Tell Psychology About the Mind." Talk delivered at The American Psychological Association, August 23, 2002; see http://www.dialogonleadership.org/docs/Rosch2002Talk.pdf

Shah, Idries. (1972). *The Caravan of Dreams.* Harmondsworth: Penguin Books.

★ Sharples, Bob. (2006). *Meditation and Relaxation in Plain English.* Boston: Wisdom Publications.

Siegel, Daniel. (2007). *The Mindful Brain: Reflection and Attunement in the Cultivation of Well-Being*. New York: W.W. Norton and Co.

Steinbeck, J. (1954). *Sweet Thursday*. New York: Viking Press.

Tolstoi, L. (1902).   *What Is To Be Done?* As translated in *The Novels and Other Works of Lyof N. Tolstoï*, edited by Nathan Haskell Dole, vol. 18.   New York: C. Scribner's Sons.

West, R. (2001). "Theories of Addiction." *Addiction* 96 (1): 3–13.

Wilson, K.G., and A.R. Murrell. (2003). "Values-centered Interventions: Setting a Course for Behavioral Treatment." In S.C. Hayes, V.M. Follette, and M. Lineham, eds., *The New Behavior Therapies: Expanding the Cognitive Behavioral Tradition*. New York: Guilford Press.

★Yangsi, Rinpoche. (2003). *Practicing the Path*. Boston: Wisdom Publications.

★Yeshe, Lama. (2000). *Wisdom Energy*. Boston: Wisdom Publications.

★Yeshe, Lama. (2003). *Becoming Your Own Therapist* and *Make Your Mind an Ocean*. Boston: Lama Yeshe Wisdom Archive.

★Yeshe, Lama. (2008). *Universal Love: The Yoga Method of Buddha Maitreya*. Boston: Lama Yeshe Wisdom Archive.

★Zopa, Lama Thubten. (1994). *The Door to Satisfaction*. Boston: Wisdom Publications.

index